The Essential Handbook of Weaving

The Essential Handbook of
WEAVING

Rosemary Murray

Bell & Hyman

London

First published in 1981 by
BELL & HYMAN LIMITED
Denmark House
37–39 Queen Elizabeth Street
London SE1 2QB

British Library Cataloguing in Publication Data
Murray, Rosemary
    The essential handbook of weaving.
    1. Hand weaving.
    I. Title
    746.1'4   TT848

ISBN   0 7135 1282 2

Dedication and Acknowledgements

This book is dedicated to my husband for his unfailing encouragement and for supplying the photographs. Thanks are due to Maggie Riegler, Fiona Mathison and the Weavers of the Martinerie for allowing me to show their work and to Mr R. Oddy for permission to reproduce *Old School Tie* by Archie Brennan. Figures 6, 7 and 8 from Chapter 23 are taken from *The Technique of Weaving* by Else Regensteiner, © 1970 Litton Educational Publishing Inc., reprinted by permission of Van Nostrand Reinhold Company. I would also like to thank my many students, past and present, particularly Sarah Ashman, Marissa Hardy, Susan Hosken and Ruth Lubel who lent me their hands and skill for the photography.

Photoset in Melior and printed in Great Britain by
M. & A. Thomson Litho Ltd, East Kilbride, and bound by
Hunter & Foulis Ltd, Edinburgh, for the publishers Bell & Hyman Limited.

Contents

1
Introduction to weaving

Weaving is the interlacing of two components at right angles to each other—the warp and the weft. The thickness and characteristics of the construction depend on the materials from which it is made. It can be stiff, capable of standing on its own as in basketry, or pliable as in cloth. The foundation, the warp, must be held in some way so that the weft can be interlaced. A simple fence can be made by pushing sticks into the ground and interweaving others across them. This was something primitive weavers discovered when experimenting with the natural materials available. To weave in the round strong willows or reeds were lashed together centrally, bent upward to form the ribs or warp of a basket on which the weaving was done. When the baskets were lined with skin or clay they could be used as cooking pots. Fragments of clay linings have been found which show the imprint of plain and twill weave cloth. No tools were needed.

Weaving came before cloth making. When skill in construction through weaving was being developed man was still wearing skins. Textiles began with the discovery of how yarn could be made by drawing out the fibres from a mass of wool or flax and twisting them together. The resulting yarn was longer than anything that had been used before and was also softer so that it needed a support to hold the warp in order to weave. This support was a loom and with it began the whole history of textile machinery.

The yarns which were used by these early weavers depended on what was available—wool on the back of a sheep or goat; plants like cotton and flax; or silk, richly glowing thin filaments, the natural product of the silk worm. The first to be used were flax and wool.

As soon as you begin to weave you will be faced with the choice of yarn, so it is essential to know something about what is available before you start.

YARNS FOR THE HAND WEAVER

Yarns for hand weaving come from many sources and are generally classified by the fibre present. There are natural and synthetic sources; the natural can be divided into two groups, vegetable or animal; synthetic yarns can be made partly from natural matter or be totally man-made. It is the way in which the fibre behaves on a loom that determines its suitability for weaving. The length of the fibre, the way in which it has been twisted in spinning, any processes such as mercerization to which it has been subjected, all have an effect on cloth.

Natural fibres

Cotton   This comes from the seed hair boll of the cotton plant and is a most useful yarn for the hand weaver, being strong and easy to handle. For warp and weft a wide variety of colours and thicknesses can be obtained and it can be bought in small quantities. Mercerization, treatment with caustic soda, improves its dye absorption and makes it stronger still and shiny. It can be used satisfactorily as a warp with a wool weft for upholstery. It is not as elastic as wool but is ideal for the beginner as it is easy to use and any mistakes in the weave are quickly detected as the pattern shows very clearly.

Linen   This comes from the stem of the flax plant and is a bast fibre. Linen is a difficult yarn to use as it lacks elasticity which can cause tension problems. Despite its strength the warp should be a plied yarn rather than a singles and its slippery springiness makes it a yarn to be tackled only after using other yarns successfully. It is not so readily available as cotton or wool. There are mixtures of cotton and linen intended for hand knitting which are quite useful for weaving also.

Wool This is the animal fibre obtained from sheep.

Wool is the weaver's favourite being easy to use, pliable and elastic with a character of its own. Virgin wool is new wool, the strongest; reclaimed or reprocessed wool is made from materials shredded and respun into yarn. The properties of the yarn depend on the staple length and the way in which the yarn is spun.

Woollen yarn is made from carded fibres that are comparatively short and jumbled together in the spinning to make a soft bulky yarn. 'Spun in oil' means that they contain some of the natural fleece oils or added oils for the spinning process. This may deaden the colour but will vanish after washing and fulling (see p. 147). Tweeds are singles yarns in oil.

Worsted Worsted is made from longer stapled fibres which are combed so that they lie parallel to each other and make a smooth strong yarn with no oil left in it.

Silk This is a natural filament from the silk worm. Silk can only be used by an experienced weaver. It is expensive and not easily obtained. fine and very difficult to use. It can be made stronger by plying, then it is known as thrown silk.

Synthetic yarns These can be part vegetable or protein or totally man-made. There is a large range of synthetic fibres made from different substances, wood, coal, petroleum, casein being

examples. Some have been subjected to processing which gives them an additional texture that they would otherwise lack. They were originally made to imitate the natural protein filament produced by the silk worm, the first synthetic produced in the late nineteenth century was called artificial silk rather than rayon. Today synthetics are taken at face value, their properties being their own; some of their characteristics help the weaver, others may hinder. Certainly their cheapness, strength, availability and wide range of brilliant colours make them attractive.

FANCY YARN (Fig. 1.1)
Most fancy yarns are intended to be used as weft alone. Some can be used for warps but must be tested to see if they would stand the tension and the constant rubbing of the reed against the threads. Fancy yarn can be used in conjunction with a fine smooth yarn, warping the two together and using them as one. Some textured yarns are formed by plying together a firm core and a soft, purely decorative yarn, while others are the result of plying together a fine and a coarse yarn. Others are made textured by the way they are spun, sometimes tightly then with hardly any twist at all. They are available in natural, synthetic or mixed fibres. They can add spice to a dull warp; a small range of fancy yarn is essential to the serious weaver.

S OR Z TWIST IN YARNS (Fig. 1.2)
Yarns where the fibres lie in the diagonal line like the centre of an S from left to right are known as S twist. Most singles woollens are these. Z yarns are those where the direction of the diagonal is reversed, right to left as in a letter Z. The angle of twist varies depending on the number of twists. This controls the yarn strength and affects the

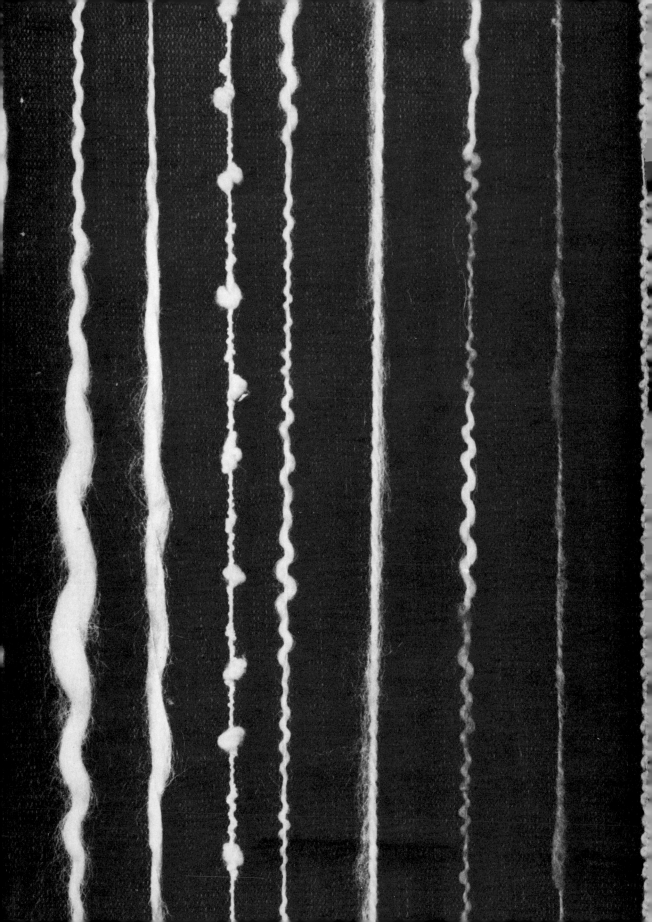

Fig. 1.1   Fancy yarns

appearance of the cloth. A slight twist makes a loosely spun yarn and a softer fabric while a highly twisted yarn will make a stiffer cloth.

Plied yarns can be of the same twist or a combination of S and Z. They have an influence on the clarity of pattern. In twill pattern the diagonal pattern line is more pronounced if the warp and weft are of opposite twist.

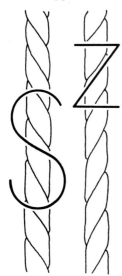

Fig. 1.2   S and Z twist

Packaging and suppliers   Collecting yarn comes naturally to the hand weaver, one develops 'magpie' tendencies to gather some here and there. Recognized stockists are the best source, they know their trade and their yarns have the qualities needed. Cottons can be purchased in very small quantities. Woollens tend to be sold in larger amounts which may mean that building up

a store can be expensive. Yarn left over when you have finished a project is never wasted, you will always find a use for it. The range of colours offered is wide but, if economy is a necessity, buy undyed yarn and dye it at home. Thick wool in a variety of colours can be bought from carpet mills. When ordering, it is as well to say that the yarn is for weaving to avoid cut hanks being put in to make up the exact weight. Knitting machine yarn shops are another source. Most suppliers have a system of credit on large cones bought. When returned to the shop, the amount left on the cone is credited against your next purchase. Woollens may not be strong enough for warps but can certainly be useful for wefts.

Yarns are packaged in various ways, some on spools wound on a plastic or cardboard tube which revolves to unwind, others on cops or cones, the yarn unwinding from the top, a few yarns are sold in skeins.

A collection of yarn, oddments of left over knitting wools, unravelled sweaters, string, strips of old sheeting, tights, all dyed in the same dye bath will often yield surprising results. A weaver must know something about the classification of yarns in order to be able to order from a catalogue with confidence. If the following pages seem too technical for you, leave them until you need to read them for reference.

THE COUNT OF YARN

The count is a system of classifying a yarn according to the relationship between the weight and length. In a fixed weight system yarn is measured by the number of hanks of a certain length which go to make up a 1lb weight. For example, in cotton, a yarn designated as having a count of 1 would contain one hank of 840 yds in 1lb weight. This would be a thick yarn. A finer

9

yarn would be a 4, that means that there are four hanks each 840 yds long in each 1lb weight. This is when the yarn is single. If it is plied, this information is included in the count, e.g. 2/4s means that a yarn of the size of 4 has been folded double when plied; the ply and yarn are separated by a line. By plying the yarn it has doubled in thickness so that it virtually becomes the same in terms of thickness as a yarn with a count of 2. Another example is 3/18s and 2/12s which are plied from two yarn sizes but the plying has made them both the same thickness., a count of 6. Slightly different yarns are 2/4s and 2/6s, the first a little thicker than the second. The count of the basic yarn is divided by the number of strands in the ply.

The unit measurement making up the pound weight varies with the classification of yarn:
cotton—hank 840 yds
linen—lea 300 yds
spun silk—hank 840 yds
worsted—hank 560 yds

Woollens vary according to the place of origin:
Galashiels—cut 240 yds
Yorkshire—skein 256 yds
West of England—hank 320 yds

Synthetics (spun like cotton)—hank 840 yds
Most synthetics are extruded to form a filament from a man-made substance as in the natural processes of the silk worm. In these the unit of classification is length. Yarns are labelled high for coarse yarn and low for fine.

Tex system of yarns Tex is the international system of classifying yarns. It is a fixed length system—the weight of 1000 metres of yarn in grammes. It is a direct system in that the length,

1000 metres, is weighed and if it weighs 15 grammes the Tex count is 15. As with cotton any plying must be included in the labelling so that the plied size comes first. R 30 Tex/2 means that two of the single yarns of 15 count have been plied together to make a yarn twice as thick. As the yarn gets thicker, the number rises.

This is completely opposite to the fixed weight system which depends on the number of lengths of yarn, hanks, there are in 1lb. The count number grows smaller as the yarn gets thicker.

Although Tex is the international system, most stockists still use the fixed weight system. If you know the length of yarn you are buying it is easier to plan your work. In a warp the length of one end multiplied by the total number of ends in the warp will give the length of yarn needed. Because of loom wastage, you will not need quite so much for the weft. A sample piece of the cloth woven to so many inches will help you calculate the total weft length needed.

2
Improvized looms

You do not have to buy a loom before you can start weaving. All sorts of makeshift looms can be made very simply. Strips of card pinned out on a board with others interlaced at right angles can be used to explore pattern forms. Cardboard with notches cut in the opposite edges can support a warp. A simple project which could be attempted by young children is using a plastic tray (like those used in supermarkets to package food) as an improvized loom.

SUPERMARKET FOOD TRAY LOOM
Warp threads are the foundation for the cloth and are stretched tightly across the loom. The weft thread is interlaced over and under the warp threads to make cloth. Let's start with plain weave, which is like darning.

You will need:
Some thick 4-ply or double-knitting wool or nylon,
Wide Sellotape,
A plastic supermarket meat tray,
A tape measure,
A pair of scissors,
A needle with an eye large enough to take the yarn (a second longer needle with a curved tip is used in the photographs to weave with but this is not essential).

WEAVING ON A SUPERMARKET MEAT TRAY

Make a loom from the tray:
1. Use the Sellotape to bind the two shorter edges, top and bottom, of the tray. Do this twice. Lap three-quarters of the tape over the front first. Then with the second piece of tape lap three-quarters over the underside. This will strengthen the edge into which you will cut slits and pierce holes to hold the warp threads.

Fig. 2.1   Cutting slits in the top edge

2. Holding a tape measure along the top edge, cut small slits along the tray at $\frac{2}{10}$ in (0·5 cm) intervals (Fig. 2.1). Do the same at the opposite bottom edge. Make sure that you start the cuts at the same distance from the side of the tray at the bottom edge. Your slits must be *exactly* opposite one another. Finish about 1 in (2·5 cm) from the edge of the tray.
3. Halfway between the first two slits and about $\frac{1}{2}$ in (1·3 cm) below them, pierce a hole with the needle. Pass the needle right through the plastic to make sure the hole will be big enough to take the wool (Fig. 2.2). Make a series of holes in a *straight line* between each pair of slits, finishing at the right end. Do the same at the bottom of the tray. The warp threads are going to fit into these slits and holes.

Fig. 2.2   Piercing holes between each slit ½in (1.3cm) from the edge

Fig. 2.3   Putting on the first warp thread in the two middle slits

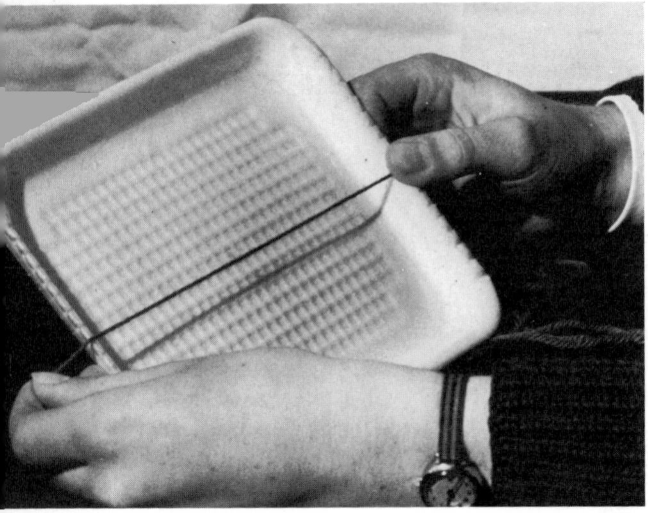

Fig. 2.4   Putting on the second warp thread between the next two holes

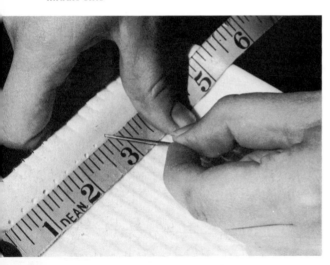

Put the warp on your loom

1. Estimate how much yarn you will need to thread *half the tray*. Measure the amount needed to take a thread from top to bottom of the tray multiplied by the number of pieces you will need. Allow a little extra and wind that amount off the ball of wool passing the needle along it. *Don't cut it off the ball*. This is to avoid knots in the warp.

2. The needle should be near the ball with the measured length pulled through it. Now, starting in the middle, press the wool into the central slits from top to bottom edge (Fig. 2.3). Return the wool to the top edge through the bottom and top holes (Fig. 2.4). Work like this until the left side of the loom is threaded. Secure the warp end under the tray with tape.

Fig. 2.6   A ruler has been passed through the space under the threads in the slits at the top of the tray. Now a strip of card is being woven under all the threads in the holes

Fig. 2.5   Threading the second half of the warp, starting from the centre

Fig. 2.7   The first row of weaving. Note the curved tipped needle is being used and is passing under the threads in the slits

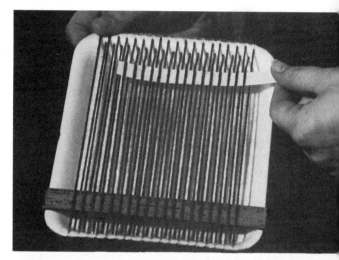

Fig. 2.6   A ruler has been passed through the space under the threads in the slits at the top of the tray. Now a strip of card is being woven under all the threads in the holes

Fig. 2.7   The first row of weaving. Note the curved tipped needle is being used and is passing under the threads in the slits

3.   Estimate the yarn needed for the other half of the warp and cut it off the ball. Thread it on to the needle and starting in the centre complete the right side of the warp, securing the end underneath with tape (Fig. 2.5). There will be eight threads to every 1 in (2·5 cm).
4.   There will be a space under all the threads held in the slits. Pass a small ruler through this at the top of the loom. Weave a narrow strip of card under the threads in the holes and over those in the slits. Push this strip to the bottom of the tray. It will give you a firm edge to weave on and improve the tension of the warp (Fig. 2.6). Your loom is now ready to use.

WEAVING
Thread your needle with the same kind of yarn, using a contrasting colour. Use a long piece of wool to avoid joining in a new weft end too soon.

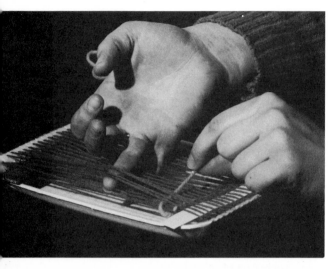

Fig. 2.8 *Finishing off the loose ends of the first row*

Fig. 2.9 *Weaving the second row by passing the needle under the threads in the holes and over those in the slits*

Fig. 2.10 *The second row of weaving. The yarn is being pulled through to form an arc from side to side while the right edge is held out to stop the side being drawn in*

First row of weaving This is made by passing the wool under all the threads in the slits. Because there is a space there, this is easy to do so start from the left side if you are right-handed (Fig. 2.7). If left-handed, weave the first row from your right. Pull the yarn through until a short length is left sticking out at the side. Tuck this end in by turning it round the end warp thread and back under a few warps (Fig 2.8). A row of weaving is called a pick.

Second row Weave the thread under the warps in the holes and over those in the slits (Fig. 2.9). This is where the needle with the curved tip is useful. When taking the weft across, hold the edge of the warp out so that they cannot draw in

Fig. 2.11 *This is wrong. The weft thread has been pulled across too tightly, causing the edge to draw in*

Fig. 2.13   Joining in a new weft thread

(Fig. 2.10). Let the weft make a loose arc in between the warp threads (Fig. 2.10). Pick this arc down with the needle point starting in the middle (Fig. 2.12). This is called beating the weft. The ruler which is at the top of the loom (under the warp threads in the holes) can be moved smoothly down to the bottom and used to beat the rows as well. With a wool warp friction may cause little pieces of wool to fluff out on the warp strands making it difficult to pull the weft across. Beating with the ruler will clear the space and allow the weft to pass through it.

Fig. 2.12   Picking down the arc in the second row with the needle point

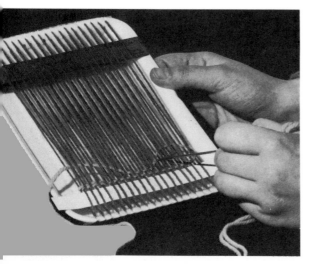

How to join a new length of yarn   Use the old yarn as far as you can. Insert the new yarn of the same colour into the weaving making sure that the threads overlap. Do this near the side edge of the cloth for the neatest finish (Fig. 2.13). The loose ends can be cut off close to the weaving.

When you have finished, cut through the stitches of yarn which occur on the under side of the edge of the tray and pull your cloth off the loom. The tray can now be used again.

15

3

Frame looms

With the experience gained by using the simplest plastic tray loom, you are now ready to go on to larger pieces of cloth using a frame. This should not be expensive as you can find old frames in the house or at a jumble sale. You will be handling a longer length of yarn, using two knots, which you will also use later on, and making leashes to form one of the sheds for weaving.

Any strong rectangular frame which is properly squared up can be used, an old picture frame, an old-fashioned clothes airer or a deckchair frame can support a warp. It should be clean and it may be necessary to sandpaper it so that there are no rough places to catch the yarn. It should be larger than the weaving planned as you will not be able to weave right up to the top and bottom or close to the edge at each side.

Artists' stretcher frames are ideal as they can be adjusted with small wooden wedges to tighten the tension.

WINDING ON THE WARP

A warp with a good tension is the foundation of good cloth. There are several ways to warp a frame. Use a coarse cotton, the kind that is knitted into dishcloths, with six or seven threads to 1 in (2·5 cm).

A figure of eight wrap Make marks every 1 in (2·5 cm), along the top edge starting a little distance from the side. Tie on the cotton yarn and wind it from the top to the bottom in a continuous figure of eight wrap. As the yarns pass one another, they will form a cross which will keep them in their correct place. Try to wind evenly and parallel to the edge. Finish with a firm knot at the bottom edge.

Circular warping If the warp is taken right round the frame it will form two layers of threads and double the length on which to weave. An independent cloth can be made on each side on one cloth, double the length, the warp being moved carefully round the frame bringing the bottom layer to the top. Tie on the yarn at the top and wind smoothly round. No cross forms with this method.

Tying the warp on in pairs Another way is to tie the warp on in pairs. Cut the yarn two and a half times the length of the frame, fold in half and tie to the top with a lark's head knot (Fig. 3.1).

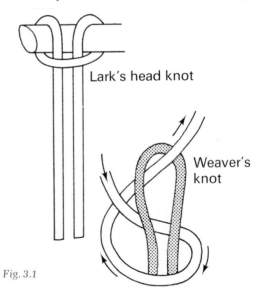

Lark's head knot

Weaver's knot

Fig. 3.1

Fig. 3.2 *Warp tied on in pairs. Simple frame, making the shed with shed stick, twining at top and bottom, bracing strings attached to the frame sides*

Fig. 3.3 Making the countershed with leashes on a leash rod

Stretch the two threads down to the bottom, over the top of the bottom edge. Divide them underneath bringing one warp up at each side (Fig. 10.12). Tie with a double knot over the two threads. Although this method takes longer it makes a very firm tension with no slipping at all. The two knots learnt are used in later processes in the book. No cross is formed (Fig. 3.2).

Winding the warp between the nails A strong frame is needed for this method as the nails must not go through the frame. Holes drilled into the wood with the two rows a small distance from each other will avoid splitting the wood. Take the thread over two nails. A closer set warp using finer yarn can be made by winding the yarn round one nail.

PAIRING
As there is no reed to set the warp threads equidistant from one another, a pairing or twining thread is worked in warp yarn from one side of the frame to the other. Cut a length of yarn four times the width of the frame and fold it in half. Attach it with a lark's head knot to the left side of the frame. Twist the two folds of yarn round one another until you reach the first warp strand. Continue the twining weave across the warp, enclosing each strand of warp in a twist of the twining yarn. Work twining across the warp at the top and at the bottom (Figs. 3.2 and 5.6).

THE SHED STICK
Insert a flat stick under every other warp thread at the top of the frame; this is called a shed stick. Its first function is to act as a tensioning device and, turned on its side, the thickness of the stick will raise the threads to create a space wide enough to pass the weft yarn. The space is called

a shed. When the other threads, underneath the shed stick, are raised this is called the countershed.

To make the countershed in the same simple way is not possible as the shed stick already inserted rests on the warps which would be raised by the countershed and prevents them from rising.

Every other weft row, called a pick, must be made by darning the weft through and this is very time consuming. It would be quicker if groups of warps could be raised at the same time. The necessity to find some way to do this led primitive weavers to experiment with leashes, lengths of yarn passed under groups of warps which are not being raised by the shed stick. By pulling on the leashes the countershed can be made as easily as the shed.

MAKING LEASHES
Cut some string in pieces 12 in (30·5 cm) long, fold them in half, tying the ends together, taking up the same amount of string each time. Attach them to each warp thread not being raised by the shed stick, with a lark's head knot (see Fig. 3.1). Thread all the long loops on to another stick, the leash rod. When raised this will lift every other warp to form a countershed (Fig. 3.3). After the pick has been woven the leash rod is simply laid across the warp allowing the threads to resume their original position. The loops will not slip to the back of the weaving and get in the way because they are tied to the rod. A string can be used instead of a rod.

Another way to make leashes is to make one continuous leash, passing under a warp and round the rod alternately. Work a few blanket stitches in the string (the number depending on the distance between the warps) before passing

round the next warp. A small block of wood with a cup hook at each side will form a lodging for the leash rod leaving both hands free to weave. With the loom in the upright position, pull on each of the groups of leashes in turn to open the shed to pass the weft (Fig. 3.4).

THE WEFT YARN

The weft yarn is wound into small flat skeins of yarn so that it can be passed easily through the shed. These are easily made on the fingers of the hand wrapping the yarn from the thumb to little finger in a figure of eight. Because of their shape they are called butterflies (Fig. 3.5). The loom is now ready for use.

Fig. 3.4   Using leashes to make the countershed

Fig. 3.5   Making a butterfly

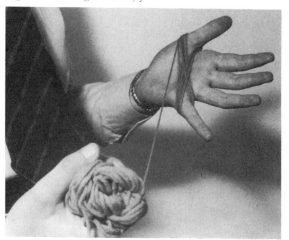

Fig. 3.6 *Making the shed with the shed stick on its edge*

Fig. 3.7 *Turning the loose end of the first pick back through the shed. A stick is being used to make a firm base for beating*

STARTING TO WEAVE

The frame can be used with its base on the lap, with the weaver sitting at a table which will provide a firm support. A very large frame is better propped against the wall.

Turn the shed stick on its edge and pass the weft, skeined into a flat butterfly, through the space the shed formed (Fig. 3.6). Turn the loose end back into the same space and press the weft row against the twining worked at the bottom of the warp (Fig. 3.7). The countershed will be made by pulling on groups of leashes in turn. Firming the rows of weaving, beating, is done with the fingers, a kitchen fork or a flat stick inserted after the weft (Fig. 3.8). Pull the stick toward you with both hands.

When weaving place the yarn in an arc in the shed and beat in so that there is enough yarn for the take-up caused as the weft bends over the warp across the cloth (Fig. 2.10). If you are drawing the weft in too much, the edge of the cloth will not be straight (Fig. 2.11). Watch this very carefully as it can happen almost without you noticing. Leaving too big an allowance for the take-up, will result in loops on the edge of the cloth.

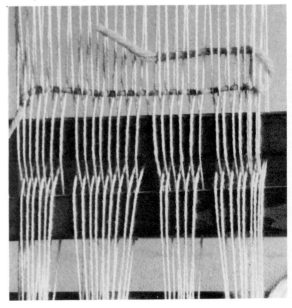

20

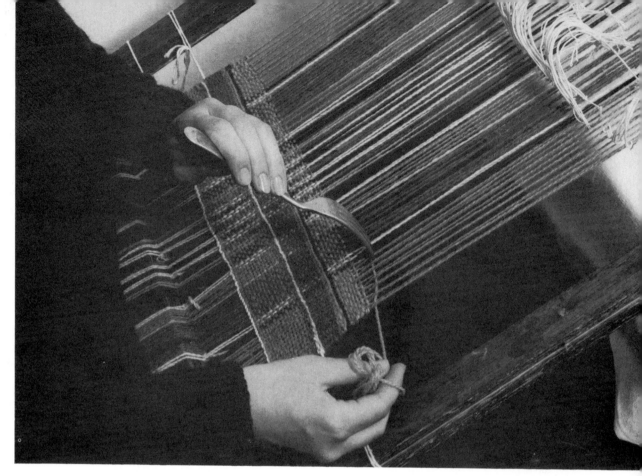

Fig. 3.8   *Frame loom: beating in the weft*

Fig. 3.9   *Joining in a weft*

WEFT JOINS
Soon you will come to the end of your yarn and
have to make a join. Try to make this at the side
of the cloth rather than in the centre and overlap
the old and new yarn for a few warps so that it is
double. It will not show as it is the same colour
(Fig. 3.9).

JOINING IN A DIFFERENT WEFT COLOUR
Because of the change of colour take the end of
the old colour back into the same shed. Start at
the opposite side with the new colour and finish
the tail back into the first shed of new colour
after you have woven the row.

WHAT CAN YOU WEAVE?
With a frame, plain weave is the cloth that can be
made. Try out some of the techniques described in
the section on plain weave. Any of them will
make interesting work; tapestry is also suitable
for frame loom weaving.

Fig. 4.1 Backstrap loom

4
The rigid heddle

This section introduces the rigid heddle, a simple yet ingenious device used for centuries by weavers to make the two sheds easily without the use of shed sticks and leashes. In a sense it becomes a loom; using it, weaving can be worked on any shape deep enough to depress the heddle. It can be used with a frame to speed up the rate of work. On its own, with the simple addition of rods at front and back to hold the warp it forms a backstrap loom. New techniques to be learnt are threading the heddle making it into a back strap loom and using the heddle.

The rigid heddle consists of a length of wood or metal cut into a series of slots or slits with holes in the middle of the strips which come between them. The warp ends are placed one in the hole and one in the space. When the heddle is raised, with the warp taut, the warps held in the holes must rise with it. The other ends will occupy the bottom of the spaces in between the strips, thus making a shed. The countershed is made by pushing the heddle down; warp ends in the spaces will now be at the top of the heddle. Rigid heddles can be made in wood, or metal ones bought quite cheaply in various different sizes.

THE BACK STRAP LOOM
Using a rigid heddle of up to 15 in (43 cm) width, the back end of the warp is tied to any convenient hook or door handle or clamped to a table. The front end is tied to the weaver behind his back, the tension of the warp being regulated by the weaver (Figs. 4.1 and 4.2). It is a cheap way to start weaving and the work has the advantage of being portable; when you have finished you can roll the loom up, put it in a drawer or hang it on a wall. Rigid heddles are usually set to take fairly coarse threads at 13 to 1 in (2·5 cm).

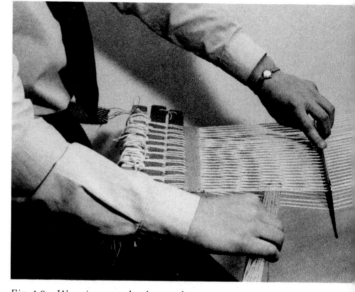

Fig. 4.2 Weaving on a backstrap loom

Making a warp for a backstrap loom The way in which the holes and spaces are cut in the rigid heddle determines the number of threads to 1 in (2·5 cm) in the warp. When woven, 13 threads will make just under 1 in (2·5 cm). This will help you decide how wide you will make the warp. The length of warp which can be successfully handled with a backstrap loom is limited so make a warp of 1 yard (1 metre). With wastage for tying on to the front rod and the small length at the back of the warp that cannot be used, this should give you a workable length. The warp must not be too thick, 2/4s or 2/6s cotton would be suitable or a medium crochet cotton. Cut a length of 2 yards (2 metres); folded in half this will

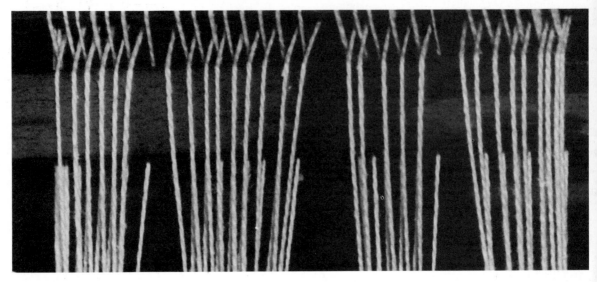

Fig. 4.3   Order of warp threads

make two warps. Put the lengths on to a warp stick in pairs with a lark's head knot. Lay the completed warp flat on a table and make a cross in the threads by weaving two flat sticks under and over the warps in opposite fashion. Push the cross sticks, as these are called, up the length of warp and tie them together, put a rubber band round one stick end and twist it before slipping it on to the other stick. Clamp the stick holding the warp to the table.

Threading the rigid heddle   Weight the warp along its length with a heavy object to stop it slipping about. The heddle must be held still also for threading. The best way to do this is to tape it to the table top with the holes above the table level or wedge it between two heavy yet slim books.

First, look carefully at the way in which the warp threads come from the cross sticks; one comes over and one under the stick nearest to you (Fig. 4.3). You must maintain this order when you are threading the heddle. If you are not using the full width of the heddle, start threading from the middle so that the warp will be properly centred.

Find the thread with your left hand and hold it between the thumb and the first two fingers so that it is taut. With the hook upwards, pull on the taut part of the thread bringing it through the central hole towards you. Thread each hole and space at each side finishing with a double thread in the end hole and space. This will make a strong edge, the selvage. When you have finished threading tie up the warps in groups in front of the heddle so that they do not slip back while you are attaching the warp to the front rod.

Making the heddle into a loom   You will need a belt or a piece of webbing as a backstrap and another stick to make the loom. Tie one end of the belt to the stick and pass it behind your back fastening the other ends of stick and belt together. Attach the ends of the warp to the stick tied on to your waist. Use the same knot that was used at the bottom of the frame loom. It is a common knot in weaving as it is firm and easy to tighten. Take the middle group of warp threads and pass them over the front stick dividing them underneath and bringing one half up at each side. Tie with a single knot. Then take the outside group at each edge and then all the other groups of warps. Tension the knots by pulling on the ends of the yarn and, holding the tension, make another knot on top of the first.

You are now ready to start weaving. The two sheds will be made by raising and depressing the heddle, the tension can be tightened by leaning back on the warp.

Start by raising the heddle and inserting a stick in the shed made. Lower the heddle and insert another stick in the countershed. This will help to spread out the warp and give a firm base for the weaving. Then using a butterfly of yarn or a shuttle begin to weave, raising and lowering the heddle alternately (Fig. 4.4), trying to make a good edge and beating the weft in evenly (Fig 4.6). Remember to lean back slightly on the backstrap to keep the warp taut (Fig. 4.2).

As you progress up the warp you will come to a point when the weaving edge, the fell edge, is too far away from you to be comfortable. Remove the backstrap from your waist, roll the two sticks forward and tie a flat rather wider stick under the roll of cloth and sticks to hold it in position. Then retie to the waist and proceed.

This is a simple technique yet it is one which involves much skill to be done well. It is a remarkably versatile and portable form of weaving, involving a basic rhythm which needs much practice to perfect. Any of the plain weave based techniques in the next section can be made with it.

Fig. 4.4   Backstrap loom with the rigid heddle. Depressing the heddle

Fig. 4.5   Placing the weft in the shed in a loose arc to allow for take-up

Fig. 4.6   Beating the weft in with the fingers

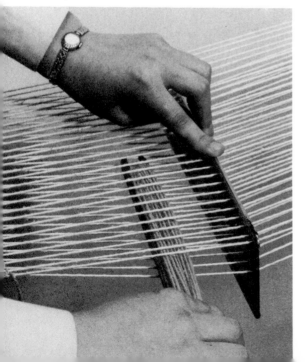

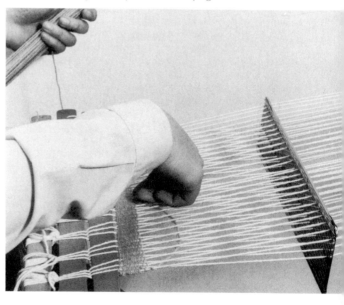

5
Plain weave

An understanding of this simple weave is the foundation of skill in the craft. Perhaps the word 'plain' suggests a dull fabric, but this is not so. It was certainly the first weave ever used: museums are full of rich, interesting fabrics worked in this simple weave. Despite the number of patterns possible on a shafted loom, plain weave is still used more than any other pattern today. It can be made on any loom, the simplest and the most sophisticated. The warp and weft interlace singly, the only weave in which this happens.

USING PLAIN WEAVE
Every other warp end is raised and the weft yarn passed under them. In the countershed the opposite warp ends, over which the weft passed in the first pick, are raised and the weft passed under them. This simple and unique interlacing of warp and weft makes a strong cloth less elastic than other weaves. Woven in thick yarn it can make sacking and yet the same weave is used to make fine silks. It is challenging to use, there is no surface pattern to disguise faults—one of the most difficult cloths to make well is plain weave worked with a dark weft on a white warp.

BALANCED PLAIN WEAVE
This is made when there is the same number of picks to warp ends. When the warp and weft are of equal thickness, the vertical and horizontal take-up will be the same. Another name for this is a 50/50 cloth.

RAISING A SURFACE TEXTURE
There are several ways of raising a surface texture on plain weave. The simplest is to weave with a fancy yarn such as a gimp, bouclé or slub (Fig. 5.1). Raw unspun fleece can be used, worked on every pick with a supporting weft on

the alternate picks to make a firm cloth with a deep textured surface (Fig. 5.2).

Fig. 5.1   Texture caused by weft yarn, slub

Fig. 5.2   Unspun fleece as weft

VARIATION ON PLAIN WEAVE

Although the weave will be the same, a different cloth will result if thick and thin warps or wefts are used. Warps can be grouped together by threading them double or treble, or spaces can be left empty making a cloth of varying density. This can be across the whole width of cloth or occur only in certain places. The grouping and spacing can be gradual or sudden, can be all in one colour or linked to colour changes in a striped warp. The weft can follow the same variations as the warp or not. A simple arrangement like this opens up a wide range of experiments to the weaver (Fig. 5.3).

Fig. 5.3   Spaced warp, wrapped wefts, bead weaving

WARP-FACED WEAVE

With a balanced plain weave, the same proportion of warp and weft appear on the surface of the cloth. However, if there is a high enough density of warp ends to cover the thick weft completely, only the warp yarns will show on the surface and the colour and arrangement of the warp will decide the cloth. If stripes occur in the warp, the stripes will repeat along the length of cloth. Horizontal ribs form in the cloth, the depth of the ribs depending on the thickness of the weft used. The warp needs three times the normal number of ends. Nova Scotian Drugget carpet is made this way. It is a suitable cloth for thick table mats in cotton.

WEFT-FACED WEAVE

The opposite kind of weave is weft-faced when a coarse warp is set wider with few ends to the inch or centimetre, tightly tensioned and woven firmly so that the high density of weft picks packs down over the warp, hiding it completely. The weft shows on the surface and the rib formed is vertical. The design and colour of cloth depends entirely on the weft. Tapestry and boundweave are weft-faced cloths.

REPP WEAVE

If two thicknesses of yarn are alternated across the warp and weft so that the fine picks pass under the fine ends and the coarse picks under the coarse ends the ribbed cloth made is called repp fabric. If the warp yarns are of two colours, one will show on one side and the other on the reverse. Although this can be made on a single warp loom, a better effect is made using a loom with two warp beams so that the tension of the fine threads can be increased.

Fig. 5.5 *Pick-up stick raising every fourth thread for dukagång*

PLAIN WEAVE ON A STRIPED WARP

Varying the colour of the warp in narrow or wide stripes is a simple way to form a pattern. If the same order of colour is used in the weft, there will be a solid colour effect where the same coloured warps and wefts cross one another. Pin stripes in the warp, using two alternative colours and the same order of colour in the weft, will make a narrow striped cloth. Reversing the weft colour order will reverse the direction of the striped pattern. Two consecutive picks of the same colour must be woven to change the order. This is called log cabin weave (Fig. 5.4).

INLAY

Two weft threads are used, one for the cloth and a second contrasting yarn for the inlay pattern. Short lengths of inlay yarn can be woven in a random fashion or to form a regular pattern. The ends can be left on the surface to form a tuft or taken under the fabric when not in use. If the pattern occurs in the same part of the weaving, there will be a build up because the yarn will be double where the pattern is woven. It will be necessary to weave extra ground picks in between the areas of pattern to compensate for this. Simple shapes can be woven directly but more complicated designs should be worked out on squared paper.

DUKAGÅNG

A variation of inlay is where a pick-up stick is used to raise every fourth thread across the warp, the thicker pattern threads lying over the intermediate three warp ends (Fig. 5.5). A plain binder, ground yarn, the same thickness as the warp, is woven between pattern rows. The name means 'straight little paths in the cloth'.

CHAINING

This makes a series of chain loops like a crochet line on top of the fabric (Fig. 5.6). It can be made of thick yarn and is useful for outlining shapes and emphasizing curves. To work a chain the weft yarn lies under the warp but is pulled up with the fingers between the warps so that the weft interlocks with itself across the surface of the fabric. Chaining is worked from left to right on alternate picks, the yarn being returned to the left selvage with a plain pick. There should be some picks of plain weave on each side to make a firm ground underneath the pile.

CROSS CHECK

Warp colour changes of differing widths, combined with the same order in the weft, make a checked cloth. Where yarns of the same colour in warp and weft cross, solid colour will form. With

Fig. 5.4 *Log cabin*

a balanced weave there will be a pleasant effect where warp and weft colour is different.

FINGER MANIPULATED WEAVES

Using plain weave there are ways in which the threads can be manipulated with the fingers to make an interesting cloth. The origins of these techniques lie centuries ago in cultures as diverse as Persian, Turkoman, Scandinavian or Navajo. Some techniques raise a pile and others will make a lacy openwork cloth. The first two use an extra thread to make a pattern.

TWINING

Twining is a basketry technique but it has been widely used in decorative cloth making (Fig. 5.6). It is worked on a closed shed. The double weft encloses the warp thread crossing between the warps, the two threads of the double yarn passing alternately over and under the warp strands. Twining can be worked over and under two, three or more warp ends at a time and can be worked from left or right. As two wefts are used they can be of a different colour and can change places depending on whether weft threads take a full or half turn between the warps. A full turn will result in the same colour showing all the time on the top surface. Using a half turn the colours will alternate. At the edges the two warps have to cross one another to turn back into the weave.

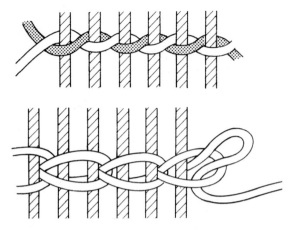

Fig. 5.6   Pairing or twining (top)   Chaining (bottom)

LOOPS

As the weft lies under every other warp strand, a simple way to raise surface texture is to pull the pattern thread up in loops where it passes over the opposite warp threads (Fig. 5.7). The next weft thread is left undisturbed in the shed, making a firm cloth. The picks must be well beaten in as this is what keeps the loops in place; they are not knotted into the fabric. To work, introduce the pattern yarn into the shed but do not beat it in. Leave the end hanging from the right edge as it is turned in on the second pattern row. With the fingers or a threading hook pull the pattern weft to the surface, slipping a double-ended knitting needle through the loop. Continue like this across the cloth, the knitting needle lying across the warp on top of the fabric and not in the shed. The diameter of the knitting neddle will affect the size of the loops and, being constant, make them even. The loops must all lie over the needle in the same direction. A second weft is woven in the same shed to make the cloth firm. Loop patterns can raise a pile in specific design areas.

Wrapping the loops round a warp when it is raised, makes a cloth in which the loops are held more firmly in the fabric (Fig. 11.2).

SOUMAK

This is woven right side up and is like an embroidery stem stitch (Fig 5.8). The weave is worked on a closed, shed, a plain binder pick between each row of the soumak.

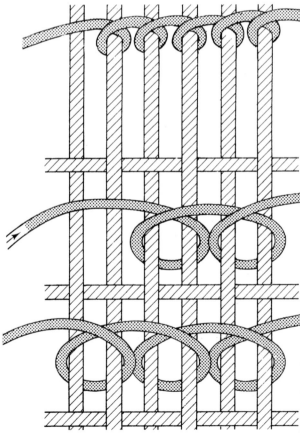

Fig. 5.8   Soumak

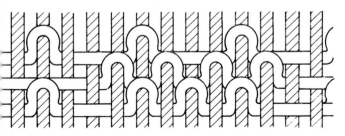

Fig. 5.7   Raising a looped pile

Fig. 5.9 Danish medallion

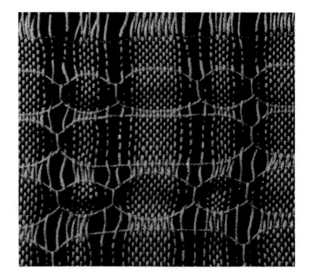

Starting from the left with the shed closed, take the pattern yarn over four and back two warps until the selvage is reached. The next pick is in plain weave in the binder yarn. Return the soumak from right to left and repeat the plain pick. Worked in opposite directions like this the lines of the weave will be opposite to one another.

To work in one direction only, making small diagonals all slanting in the same way, the weave has to be finished off at each edge and restarted at the same side each time. Soumak can be worked to form a shape or across the whole area of cloth. It is a useful weave for outlining.

FINGER MANIPULATED LACE WEAVES
A lacy fabric can be made on plain weave by various ways of moving the weft or warp ends out of their normal parallel alignment. These weaves can be done on a normal setting or on an open sett or one in which spaces are left empty in the reed. Smooth strong yarns show up the lace best.

DANISH MEDALLION
This weave groups the weft ends together to form oval shapes in the cloth (Fig. 5.9). It is best on a spaced warp using a rather fine cotton with the looping yarn in a coarser yarn of a contrasting colour or texture. Gimps, slubs and glittering yarns are effective and not too bulky.

Work in plain weave for several inches then weave one pick of contrasting yarn. Finish off this contrasting pick at each side by taking the ends back into the same shed. Decide how deep the medallions are to be and weave that number of picks in ground yarn. It is easier to draw up the weft with the yarn off the shuttle so cut off a length of the contrasting yarn, three times the width of the warp. The contrasting yarn is now reintroduced into the weave and will be used to

draw together the wefts to make the oval shape. Join in the contrasting yarn and weave, bringing it to the first space in the warp. Make a loop of the yarn and take it through the web from top to bottom below the first single pick in the contrasting yarn. Pass it vertically under the picks woven in ground yarn and bring it up on to the surface of the cloth in front of the pick you are weaving so that it makes a loop (Fig. 5.10). Take the contrasting yarn to the next space and repeat the whole process. The number and size of the drawn up medallions can vary across the width.

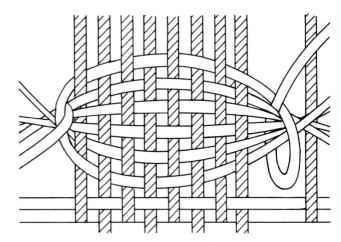

Fig. 5.10 Wrapping wefts to form lace ovals (spaced warp)

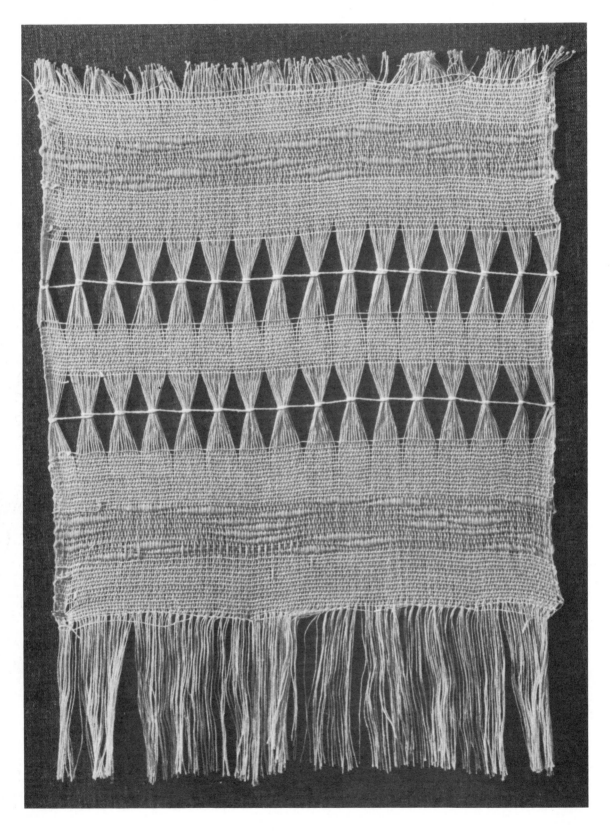

Figs. 5.11 and 5.12 (below and left) Wrapping warps

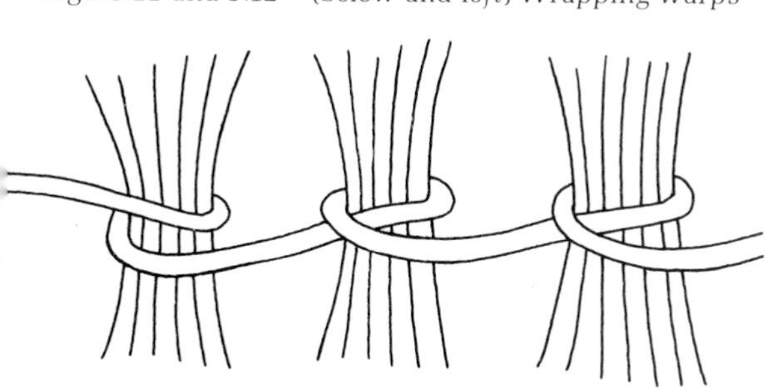

WRAPPED GROUPS OF WARP ENDS TO FORM LACE

The weft threads can be grouped together by wrapping the weft thread right round them. Having woven some picks in plain weave, with the shed closed, wrap a group of warps together with the weft yarn taking the yarn right round them in a spiral movement. Pass it across the space formed to the next group of ends and weave to the edge like this (Fig. 5.11). Some picks of plain weave should next be woven and then the wrapping repeated (Fig. 5.12).

WRAPPING WITH AN OPEN SHED

With the shed open, the pattern thread will only encompass the warps which are raised; the bottom warps will lie in their normal position. If some picks of plain weave are worked in between, the opposite warps can be wrapped the next time. This is an effective lace when used with an end and end warp of two colours alternating (Fig. 5.13).

Wrapping with a closed or open shed can be used over the whole area of warp or used in parts only. With an edge of compensating picks at the selvage it can form an openwork panel.

Groups of warp ends can be wrapped completely, the yarn finished off by threading it up underneath the wrapping and cutting off instead of taking it along to the next group. This can follow a pattern in which the little wrapped sections occur in a line or these small units of pattern can be staggered.

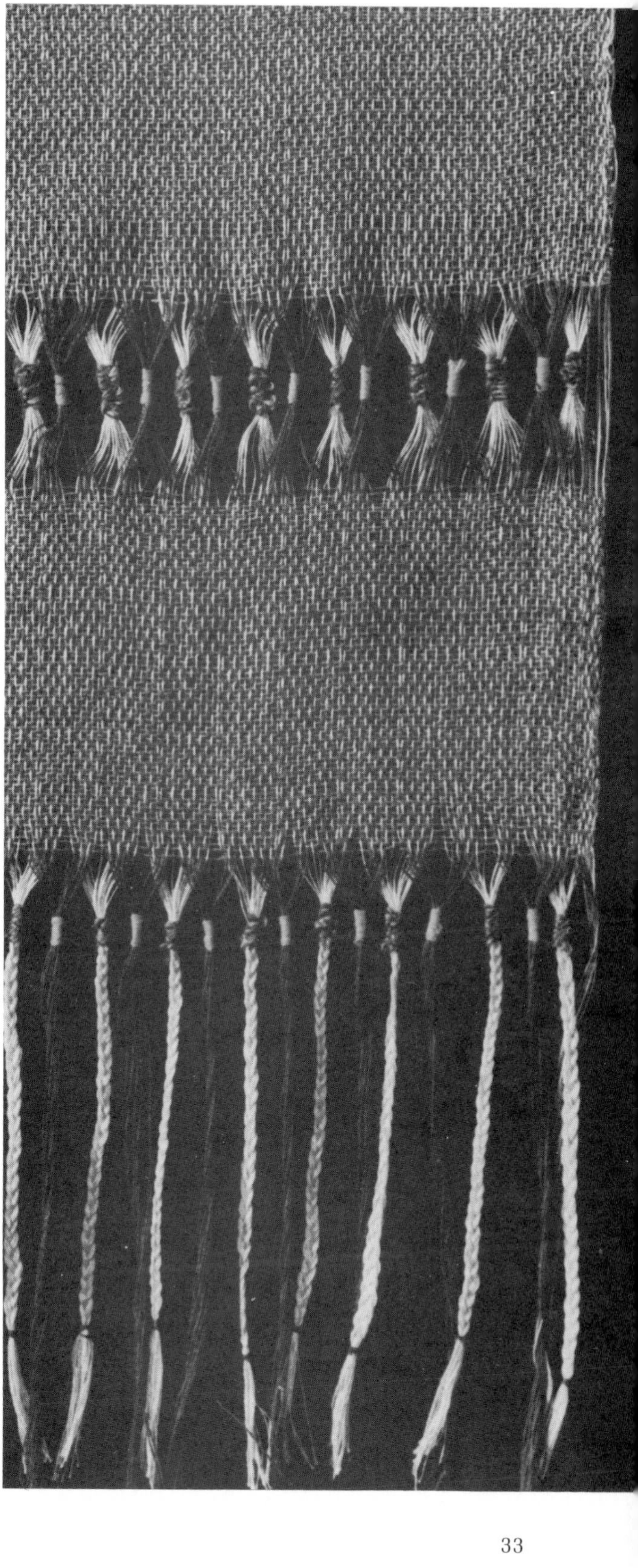

Fig. 5.13 Wrapping with an open shed (right)

Fig. 5.14 Leno lace

LENO LACE

One of the most versatile and interesting weaves to do is leno lace. In it two warps are twisted round each other and the twist which forms is made secure by the weft thread. First weave á few picks of plain weave. Slacken the tension of the loom slightly. Open the shed so that the first warp thread is on the lower level at the right edge. Starting from this edge push the top thread aside to the right and pick up the first thread from the lower level. Slip this thread on to a knitting pin or a pointed pick-up stick, then progress across the entire warp width picking up the lower warps in this way and putting them on to the pick-up stick. All the pairs of warp threads will now be twisted round one another (Fig. 5.14). When the pick-up stick is turned on its edge a weft thread can be

Fig. 5.15 Leno lace

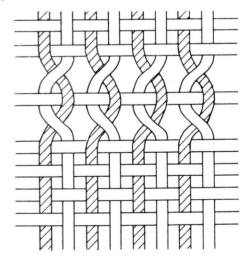

passed through the twist securing it. Beat the pick in and complete the twist by changing the shed and weaving one pick in plain weave. Leno can be worked continuously or with bands of plain weave in between the leno picks (Fig. 5.15), it can be worked on single threads or on pairs or groups (Fig. 5.16). The twists can be staggered or occur on the same groups of warp ends. Leno requires a considerable length of warp as the constant twisting of the threads causes an increase of tension.

Fig. 5.16   Leno lace

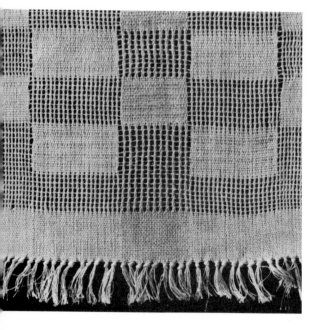

SPANISH LACE

In this weave, the weft does not pass directly from selvage to selvage but goes forward and then backwards in a series of movements (Fig. 5.17). After weaving in plain weave, decide how wide the blocks of Spanish lace are to be. If you decide, for example, that there are to be three blocks of lace in a section, take the shuttle from the right selvage to a point one third of the way across the total width of the section. Bring the shuttle out of the shed and beat in the weft using the end of the shuttle. Change the shed and weave back to the right selvage. Beat. Change the shed and this time weave across two thirds of the section. Beat.

Fig. 5.17   Spanish lace

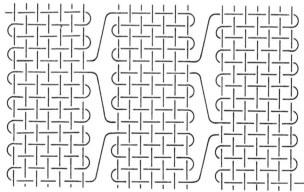

Change the shed and weave back to the beginning of this second section that is one third from the right selvage. Beat. Change the shed and complete the lace by weaving this time to the end of the section. Beat. Change the shed and weave back to two thirds across the section. Beat. Change shed and weave to the left edge of the completed section (Fig. 5.18).

Fig. 5.18   Spanish lace

Spanish lace can be woven right across the cloth or be placed in parts of it only. It looks best on a spaced warp. It can be worked in either direction. The longer wefts which pass across to the next part of the section will slope either to left or right depending on the direction in which the weave is being worked. The groups can vary in width or be the same; they can occur in the same place or be staggered.

KNOTTED PILE

Knots can be used as a fringe or as a design feature in the body of the cloth. The yarn is wound round two ends of the warp, leaving the ends of the knotted yarn to project on to the surface of the cloth to form a pile. Using short cut lengths of yarn, lay the pieces across the two warp ends, bring the ends round underneath and up between the two ends (Fig. 5.19). Tighten the knot formed by pulling the ends of the knot towards you. Knots should not be worked on the selvage ends. To make a looped pile the length should be continuous. To make a pile of uniform length work over a stick or dowel laid across the warp ends (Fig. 5.20). The knotting yarn is taken down between two warp ends and to the left, then brought over the next two ends to the right, then back to the left between them under the dowel, down between the next pair of warps, back one and over the pair, under the dowel and so on. This method can be used where all the same colour is needed in one area; the pile is then cut or can be left as loops. The knot used is called a Ghiordes from a renowned carpet weaving centre in Asia Minor.

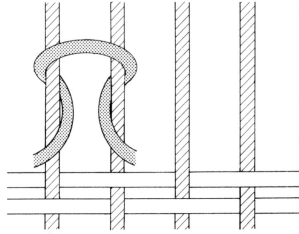

Fig. 5.19   Ghiordes knot

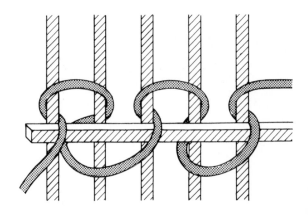

Fig. 5.20   Ghiordes knot, continuous yarn, uncut loops

6
Tapestry

Canvas embroidery is often called tapestry, but a true tapestry is woven on a loom, the design being an integral part of the cloth. What distinguishes tapestry from cloth is the way it is made. In balanced weave; warp and weft mingle on the surface of the cloth. In tapestry, the warp is set so that the weft can be beaten in to cover the warp completely.

THE LOOM FOR A TAPESTRY

Professional tapestry weavers use two kinds of looms; the high warp (*haute-lisse*), a vertical upright loom and the low warp (*basse-lisse*), a horizontal loom worked by foot power. In traditional centres of tapestry weaving, centuries-old looms are used in great ateliers and small one-family concerns (Figs.

Fig. 6.1   *Bobbins and unfinished ends*

Fig. 6.2   The design cartoon sideways under the low warp

6.1, 6.2 and 6.3). Tapestry can be woven on any loom as it is made in plain weave. A normal standard rigid heddle or shafted loom is suitable for low warp. Special two-harness vertical tapestry looms can be bought, but high warp can be made successfully on a frame. Many prefer high warp as the work can be seen easily from the back as it progresses.

WEAVING A SAMPLER
The best way to explore the possibilities of tapestry is to weave a sampler in which the techniques involved can be used (Fig. 6.4). It is the only way to find out how yarns will form a design and the various ways in which the discontinuous wefts are inserted.

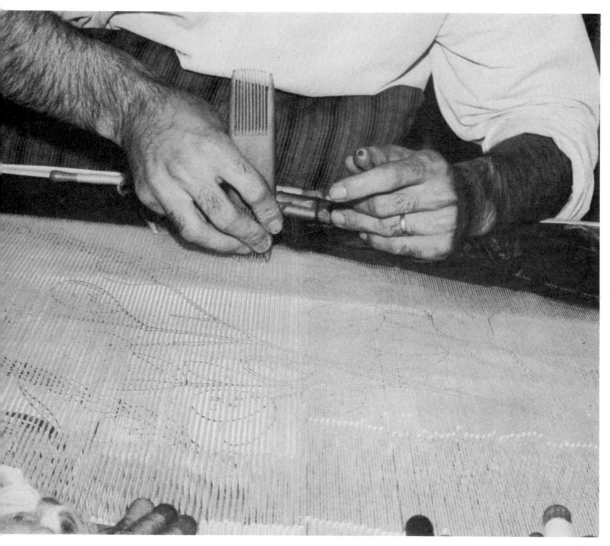

Fig. 6.3   Beating in the weft

PLANNING THE WARP

The warp yarn should be strong with a pronounced twist to withstand the strain which is put upon it and smooth so that the weft can be pushed down on to it. Any colour can be used as it is not seen in the design. Wool, cotton or linen can be used for the warp—all transfer their particular characteristics to the finished work. Linen will make a stiffer piece of work than cotton, the latter being the easiest for the beginner. The density of the warp depends on the weft which is going to be used and the design form. Between five and eight ends to 1 in (2·5 cm) is a good range to work with. The coarser sett will be suitable for very bold simple designs; eight to 1 in (2·5 cm) will mean that rather thinner wefts

and finer design detail can be used. Special tapestry warp yarn can be bought but a 2/6s yarn used double and set five doubles to the inch, or two to the centimetre will make a suitable warp for use with medium tweed yarns, 11 cut, used double, fancy yarns and thicker carpet woollens.

WEFT YARNS

Wefts in tapestry are, by tradition, wool as this is a suitably soft yarn which will pack down well to cover the warp ends completely. As colour is a very important aspect of the design, wool is a good choice as coloured wools have a vitality about them. However, synthetics and fancy yarns will give an added quality to the work.

Fig. 6.4   Tapestry sampler

STARTING TO WEAVE

Start with a heading woven in the warp yarn. This gives a firm edge on which to beat and helps to keep the weaving to its correct width. When the tapestry is finished it can be turned in or removed by pulling out.

KEEPING AN EVEN EDGE

A constant check must be kept on the edge of the work as there is a tendency for it to draw in. This is a more common fault than leaving loops at the selvage, though both are incorrect. There are several reasons why this can happen: there is a greater amount of weft take-up than in normal balanced weave as the weft bends round the warp ends, which remain straight; the weft is not continuous but is made up of small sections of different yarns; beating is done in design sections rather than straight across the whole width. All these factors contribute to the difficulty of keeping an even edge.

The tension on the warp should be even. To make sure that there is enough weft to make the turn round the warp selvage, place the weft in the shed in a series of arcs across the web, easing them down carefully into position and keeping a close watch on the selvage for any sign of drawing in. This can happen almost imperceptibly and is impossible to correct; the picks must be taken out and a fresh start made.

Keeping an even edge is a basic technique that must be mastered. Give yourself some practice in weaving in tapestry using one colour at the beginning, trying to make a firm even edge and beating the weft in so that all the warp is covered. In classical tapestry, flecks of warp showing were called 'lice' and unscrupulous ateliers used to paint them out. Make sure that there are none on your work! The weft can be used from the shuttle as it is continuous. Beat in the weft with the fingers, a fork or a flat stick inserted into the shed. Beaters can be bought; they are made of hard wood and last a long time. Experiment with the weft, using several different fine yarns together on the shuttle to build up the thickness.

USING TWO COLOURS

Select a second colour and weave in alternating picks. This will make vertical lines in the fabric. By working two picks in one colour the order of weaving the picks is reversed which will change the position of the two colours. Quite subtle and complicated arrangements can be made with this very simple technique.

Weaving several picks in one colour and then in the second colour makes horizontal stripes across the cloth.

USING BOTH COLOURS IN THE SAME SHED

The position of the two weft colours in the same shed can be changed to make a pattern of flecked or mottled patches. Use thick yarn like a carpet wool to show up the colour changes.

SKIP PLAIN WEAVE

Straight edged shapes can be made with two colours by placing each colour into the same shed where it is needed and letting it pass under the web when it is not to be seen, forming a float where it will not show. Each pick consists of two colours appearing in sections of the shed and floating underneath when not seen. This is not strictly a tapestry technique as it makes one-sided fabric with loose floats of weft on the underside. Checkerboard is woven by reversing the colour order.

Fig. 6.5   Tapestry showing vertical slit

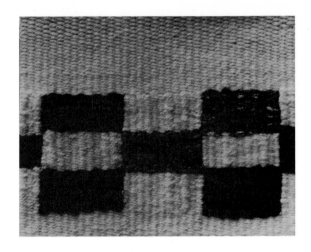

USING A DISCONTINUOUS WEFT

All the techniques described so far have involved the weft yarns passing from selvage to selvage. In tapestry, however, the yarn is not often used like this. Each pick of weft is more often made up of short lengths of yarn of different colours woven in sections according to the design. The whole craft depends on the way the wefts are treated at the colour changes. Where several different colours are to be used flat shuttles are not practical. The lengths of weft should be wound into small balls flat enough to be passed easily through the shed. Wind the yarn between the thumb and little finger in a figure of eight or a 'butterfly', finishing with a half hitch to secure it. Another way to make a flat package of yarn is to wind it simply round the fingers, the end being taken round the centre of the skein formed and finished with a half hitch to prevent it unwinding.

Tapestry bobbins can be bought but homemade ones can be improvized from the inner tubes from yarn packages with a slit cut in them to hold the end of the yarn. Lace-making bobbins make excellent tapestry shuttles.

DESIGNING

Tapestry was by tradition worked from the side, verticals becoming horizontals and all the ends left hanging on the side facing the weaver, whether low or high warp looms were being used. The right side was away from the worker. Nowadays the design determines whether the traditional method of working is used. Where there is emphasis on surface texture some weavers work with the right side towards them.

A tapestry is not a painting, it is not possible to create the effect of paint and brush strokes in a tapestry. There must be a personal response to the medium, a response which accepts the technique of the craft and its restrictions. After the basic introduction the weaver can see for himself how an image may be made. It is easy to see how much easier it is to weave a horizontal than a vertical, how very thin verticals which would involve wrapping round one warp thread are not possible and how circles are made from a series of stepped diagonals. Some weavers still work their designs from the side, while others do not; some use cartoons of their own design or the work of an artist/designer, others work directly on the loom.

USING A CARTOON

Place the cartoon directly behind the warp threads and mark the design on the warp strands with waterproof ink making sure that the mark goes right round to the back of the warp which may twist when the weaving is done.

SEQUENCE OF WEAVING SHAPES

When building up shapes it is most practical to work to the same level on the various shapes. Some you will think of as the main shapes, others will form a background. Plan carefully, working from the cartoon, the order in which the shapes should be woven without boxing in areas of warp which cannot be woven because the shed is locked. All shapes should be woven slightly higher than drawn on the design. They will pack down with the beating in of following picks.

SLITS

Vertical slit   When two different coloured yarns are woven in adjacent areas from opposite edges a vertical slit is formed where they meet and return, parallel to the selvage between the two adjacent

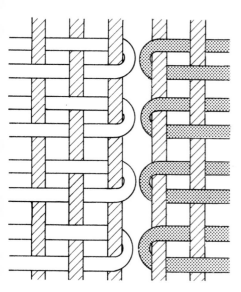

Fig. 6.6   Vertical slit

warps (Figs. 6.5 and 6.6). When only a few picks have been woven, the slit will be so small that it can be left in the fabric. Longer slits are usually sewn together afterwards unless they form a part of the design. Straight slits make the cleanest edges for sharp colour contrast, but care must be taken to ensure that the edges are straight and not pulled in.

Gothic tapestry weavers used the vertical slits formed to create their design; a damask pattern on a gown or a shadow on a fabric. In traditional Polish Khelims the slits are left forming part of the design.

Sewing the slits together   Sew the slits together using a blunt needle and taking it round the two warps where the slits occur and gently pulling them together with the stitch rather than going through the warp strands.

Using a binder thread   It is possible to use a thin thread of unobtrusive colour running in the same shed to join colours together.

Vertical dovetail   At the colour meeting point, the wefts turn round a common warp end one above another. This results in a sawed tooth edge which can be used in the design. Ridges form where the common warp end is wrapped (Fig. 6.7).

Diagonal slits   The turning point where the colours meet moves in a diagonal line. These diagonal steps may progress in single, double or more picks. This alters the angle of the meeting line (Fig. 6.8). Curves can be woven by using varied diagonal slits. As the wefts move further one way as the pattern is woven, where the colours join no slits are formed.

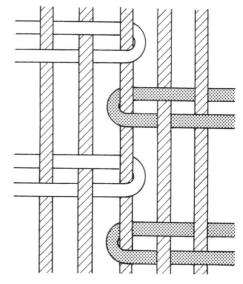

Fig. 6.7   Vertical dovetail

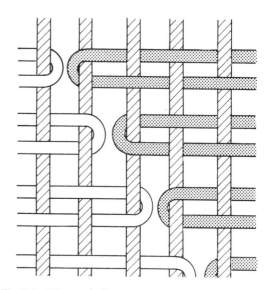

Fig. 6.8   Diagonal slit

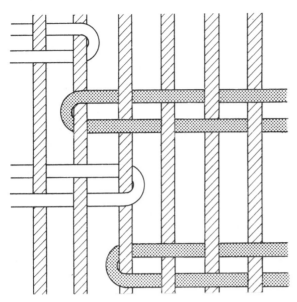

Fig. 6.9   Diagonal dovetail

Diagonal dovetail Dovetailing can be done on the diagonal; to make the angle steeper two picks of weft are needed before moving diagonally (Fig. 6.9).

INTERLOCKED WEFT
At the colour changes, the adjacent wefts wrap round each other, returning in the opposite direction in the next shed. The locking point must be central between the two warp ends. This gives clean edges to the colour changes, the underneath being the right side. It is slow to weave but the lock between the colours is very strong (Fig. 6.10).

Fig. 6.10   Interlocked weft

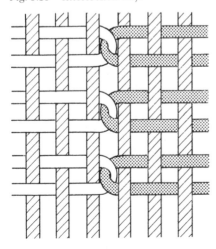

OUTLINING
To outline shapes, wrap the contrasting outlining colour round the warp end while it is raised, in the same way as for soumak, like a stem stitch. An outline can be woven round a shape which has been built up to a curved form by inserting the outlining weft and firming it closely down to the shape (Fig. 6.11).

Fig. 6.11   Tapestry outlining

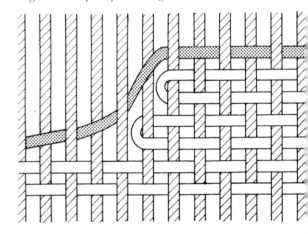

CURVED WEFT
The weft need not follow a straight line from selvage to selvage. A shape must be built up to form a small wedge or semicircle first. Instead of filling in each side with weft yarn, weave the complete pick from selvage to selvage. This pick will follow the shape below it as will the next pick. Beat with the fingers or the tip of the shuttle (Fig. 6.12).

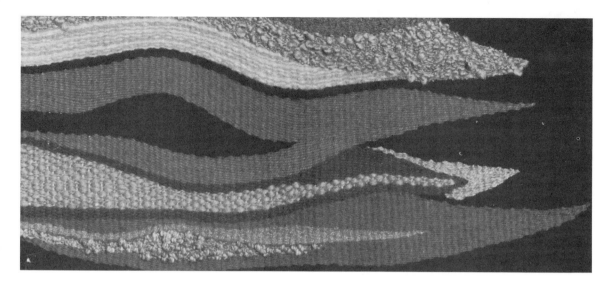

Fig. 6.12   Curved wefts

HATCHING

Colour changes produce hard edges and hatching is a way of softening an edge. It is a blending of colour lines, the weft picks. How far these colour lines go across the warp and the number of them before the next colour change can make very subtle shading effects. Colours can be made to blend into one another to form tone on a fold or enliven an otherwise dull section of the design. Half tones and blending were the delight of Gothic tapestry weavers to make the fur on a robe, folds, hair on a hunting dog, feathers on a falcon, grass in the field and the play of light on distant towers and hills. A close study of museum exhibits will show how it was done (Fig. 6.13).

Fig. 6.13   An example of hatching, Leeds Castle: Flemish tapestry. By courtesy of Leeds Castle Foundation

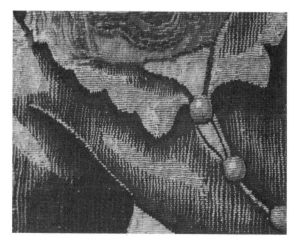

The following are examples of the work of some contemporary artist weavers in tapestry:

Archie Brennan (Fig. 6.14)

Following his initial training as a tapestry weaver, Archie Brennan has travelled widely, working and lecturing on his craft. The starting points for his pictorial weaving are taken from everyday life. Sometimes he uses a *trompe-l'oeil* effect in his work or develops a newspaper photograph or an image from a television screen. His high standard of craftsmanship translates the themes into a witty, personal view of the world.

Maggie Riegler (Fig. 6.15)

This Scottish weaver began as a painter. The initial impetus for her work is the study of natural forms. From brief pencilled designs, she works directly on to the loom, her highly textured individual style evolving from her response to the materials and techniques used. Looking at her work, one is conscious of intense areas of colour glowing against more sombre tones, pied cascades of texture which take their place in the unity of the design with flat pattern achieved by embroidery, tapestry or knitting. In the illustration *Roots*, the tapestry is stuffed and shaped to become a three-dimensional organic growth.

The Weavers of the Martinerie (Fig. 6.16)

This is the only name by which these three French weavers are known as they wish to preserve their anonymity. Their approach is philosophical, the writing of the medieval Indian sage, Kabir, forming motifs in their decorative designs. Their images are elemental: the sun, moon and stars, water, fire and earth. Their figures are stylized, recalling Assyrian, Greek and Egyptian art. Winged lions roam through paved courtyards and dark

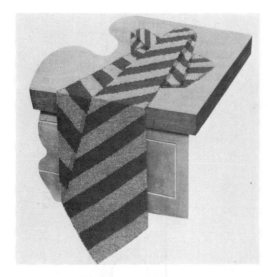

Fig. 6.14   *Old School Tie (1971) by Archie Brennan*

Fig. 6.15   *Roots (detail) by Maggie Riegler (below left)*

Fig. 6.16   *Tapestry by the Weavers of the Martinerie*

streams flow around distant towers and hills. Stained glass colours and areas of intricate detail are combined in tapestries which are woven direct with no cartoon.

Fiona Mathison (Fig. 6.17)

In tapestry, Fiona Mathison has found the perfect, flexible medium in which to create her graphic images. Her work is strong and purposeful, featuring objects found in any home—a sink, a hot water bottle or a rumpled bed. More recently, she has made telling use of profile and swarms of beautifully observed and woven insects. Her name, with that of Archie Brennan is always linked with Edinburgh, a vital centre which has played a large part in establishing fine-art weaving in Britain as a valid and internationally recognized part of contemporary art.

Fig. 6.17   *(right) Picnic by Fiona Mathison*

7
Manufactured looms

Fig. 7.1   *The Kentish two-way loom (Harris)*

Now you can weave. With the experience gained in the previous chapters, it is time to consider buying a manufactured loom. The next section on looms and additional apparatus will help you. A conventional loom is designed to help you to weave more easily and they are available in a range of sizes and types. Available space and money will influence your choice but it is a mistake to buy too narrow a loom. You need not use the whole width in experimental lengths. If the idea of pattern weaving appeals to you a simple loom would be the wrong choice. All looms must be squarely aligned and strongly constructed in stout wood to withstand the considerable strain placed upon them.

TYPES OF LOOMS

Table looms

Simple table roller looms using the rigid heddle On a frame the warp is tied directly on to the loom and the length of cloth to be made is determined by the length of the frame. Box looms are made in which the warp is still wrapped round the frame forming the foundation for the cloth but these are not very satisfactory to use as there is no way of adjusting the tension except as in a frame. A loom in which there is a roller at the front and back is a better buy; a longer length of cloth can be woven and the tension can be more easily controlled (Figs. 7.1 and 10.4). Used with a rigid heddle, a great variety of cloths based on plain weave can be made. The drawback of a rigid heddle loom is that they are limited to one sett only. Very coarse warp yarns cannot be used if too thick, as they will not divide to make the shed. Very fine yarn can be used but the cloth

will be flimsy. However, there is a wide range of fairly thick yarn, 11 cut Cheviot wool and 2/6s cotton, which are well suited to the rigid heddle. All the manipulated techniques such as leno and inlay, described in the chapter on plain weave, can be made on a simple loom and the fancy weft yarns and tied-and-dyed warps look better with plain weave. One could spend a lifetime on plain weave alone and produce a fascinating range of cloths.

A two-shaft loom with a separate reed will still only make plain cloth but the sett can be varied, which makes it more suitable for finer yarns. It is more expensive than the rigid heddle and not so quick to use. The whole point of having a shafted loom is having one with more than two shafts so that patterns can be made on it.

Table looms with shafts If the shed is made by half the warp ends rising so that the shuttle can be passed through, carrying the weft thread, the loom is said to be a rising shed loom. Most table looms fall into this category. The shafts are slung from a canopy which is attached to the sides of the frame, above the weaving. The method of suspension can be chains, which are permanent, or by strings attached to a pulley system. In most commercial looms the suspension is central and the balance must not be spoilt by housing spare heddles, not in use, at one side of the shafts. They should be placed evenly on each side.

There are several ways of raising the shafts by pulleys, levers or buttons. Where string is involved use nylon or proper loom cord, which is expensive when compared with string, but is essential unless you wish to be replacing the strings continually. They do take a great amount of strain (Figs. 7.2 and 7.3).

Fig. 7.3 (right) Harris loom on folding stand.
A = quick release device for back-roller

Fig. 7.2 (below) A four-shaft loom with one warp
beam has the same arrangement of reed and shafts.
A = canopy. B = reed in batten. C = eight shafts for
heddles. D = chains worked by side levers. E = ratchet
and pawl. F = back beams.

50

A

Table looms—the reed and tensioning The reed is carried in a batten pivoted to the sides of the loom; it swings to beat the cloth. The tension of the front and back rollers is controlled by a rachet and pawl.

Four-shafted looms With the addition of the extra two shafts a whole world of pattern weaving is opened up. Each shaft can be lifted independently or they can be raised in pairs, or threes. This, and the reed, makes possible a wide range of patterns and setts. This should be considered when buying your first loom; in terms of enjoyment alone it is well worth the price. Table looms with shafts are compact and efficient; fundamentally the same as a larger foot-operated floor loom, they take up less room and are cheaper to buy. In schools, they are ideal for teaching and experimenting; usable lengths of cloth and decorative weaving can be made on them. No complicated shuttles are needed; the simplest flat shuttle can be used quite satisfactorily.

Eight-shafted loom The more shafts a loom has the more possibilities there are for patterns of a more intricate nature. Most people find a four-shaft sufficient, but anyone understanding the four-shaft technique could easily use a loom with more shafts.

Sixteen-shafted loom This is the limit of shafts possible on a table loom and it is rather cumbersome. However, for anyone interested more in designing than in producing wide lengths, Harris Looms offer a very compact 16-shaft designer's loom.

Looms with two back beams Shafted looms with two back beams are available and are useful for cloths which need the addition of another warp. The extra beam makes the loom longer (Fig. 7.2).

Looms with special tie-ups to raise shafts in pairs These are the same as the standard type of loom except that the shafts may also be raised in pairs by means of secondary levers in much the same way that pedals operate a foot-power floor loom. This makes shaft changing quicker but the loom is a little bulkier and wider to accommodate the extra levers.

Floor looms Although the book concerns itself with table looms only, there are many different foot-operated floor looms on the market.

Horizontal floor looms Floor looms of two, four or eight shafts are available. They can have balanced, rising or sinking sheds; they can be counterbalanced or countermarched. There are different ways of attaching the shafts, through the intermediate stage of the lamms, to the foot pedals, depending on the type of loom. There are specialist books on all the processes involved (see Bibliography, p. 154). Floor looms are quicker to use with a roller shuttle than the table loom. The full aesthetic pleasure of the rhythmic sequence of treadling, throwing the shuttle and beating can be enjoyed with a floor loom. In schools they are practically unknown because of their price.

Vertical looms Floor looms can be vertical with the warp in an upright position. In this type the strong upright rug loom, with two foot-operated pedals for plain weave only, is a very sound construction. The most beautiful rugs can be made on these; either those in which the warp covers the weft completely and the whole pattern is a matter of well contrasting warp stripes; or those in which the reverse process is used, the weft beaten down to hide the warp completely. In between these two the warp and weft can show more evenly, in which case the warp colour must compliment whatever wefts are to be used.

Fig. 7.4   Masterweaver (Dryad)

Two new looms

Masterweaver: Dryad   This loom is aimed at the hobby weaver with no knowledge of weaving (Fig. 7.4). It is an upright loom with a series of warp lifting discs replacing the conventional heddles to divide the warp layers. As there is no reed, no variation of sett is possible, and as the discs are set at five-and-a-half warps to 1 in (2·5 cm) only a coarse yarn is suitable for weaving. To warp the loom the frame is rotated on its stand, the warp thread being wound on between the discs of the cylinder. Each disc has four notched position marks raised on the outer rim numbered, 1, 11, 111, and 1111 (1, 2, 3 and 4). These can be rotated individually and locked on the shaft according to the pattern chosen. A pattern control wheel at each end turns the complete cylinder to eight different positions, forming the shed. Weaving is done with a flat shuttle which also serves as a beater. There is a tension adjuster at the top of the frame. As a length of weaving is completed, a new length of warp is drawn forward.

The Kentish two-way loom: Harris   This is a roller loom aimed at the beginner and suitable for making small pieces of cloth (Fig. 7.1). The heddle, set at 12 holes and spaces to 1 in (2·5 cm), acts as a beater and spacer. It is well-made, portable and easily threaded and would be an ideal loom on which to learn, fitting in at the simple stage of a teaching scheme. It can be folded down for storage with weaving set up on it, the front and back rollers are locked by a tensioning slot at the left side. At a very competitive price it is an attractive proposition for schools and for the weaver working at home without instruction.

8
Other equipment

Some items are essential, others are useful, but not a necessity (Fig. 8.1).

WARPING APPARATUS
So far all the warps have been made on the frame itself but, using a loom with rollers, a much longer warp than the length of the loom is now possible. To make it on the loom itself is not practical so some apparatus is necessary on which to place the threads in order in a warp. This is a continuous length of yarn with the threads crossing each other in figure of eight fashion.

Whatever the method being used to make a warp, the essentials are the same. The warp tension must be even, not too slack or too tight, and the order of threads must be safeguarded.

Warping posts The simplest, cheapest warping apparatus is a set of warping posts. These are single or double pegs of thick dowelling fixed into small blocks of wood which are clamped along the edge of a table with sturdy G-clamps (Figs. 9.1 and 9.2).

The warping frame This can be bought, or is easily made. It is merely a flat piece of wood or a rectangular frame with holes drilled into it to take dowels which can be rearranged to make various lengths of warps.

The warp is taken across the frame from peg to peg, which means that a much longer warp can be made in a more compact manner than with posts placed a long way from one another (Fig. 15.1). The frame is more convenient to use for longer warps. It is usually collapsible and can be stacked away when not in use.

The warping mill Small warping mills suitable for warps up to ten yards or metres can be bought. These fold up to a small size when not in use (Fig. 15.10).

The upright warping mill These are cylindrical frames which rotate and wind the warp along a determined track. They are expensive to buy but are useful for very long warps.

SHUTTLES
Shuttles are essential for longer lengths of yarn. They can be homemade from wood, short ones from firm card may be used. They must be smooth so that they do not catch on the warp.

Flat, stick shuttles are the simplest to fill and use. They are also the cheapest. They are slow to use compared with the roller or boat shuttle, but their simplicity and cheapness make them a good choice for a table loom (Fig. 7.1).

Boat and roller shuttles These are more complicated to fill and more expensive to buy, but are quicker to use than the flat shuttle. They work by sliding through the shed on the shuttle race and are ideal for floor looms where the feet change the shed, while the hands are free to catch and throw the shuttle. Using a table loom where the sheds are changed by hand-operated levers, the rhythm of using the roller shuttle is interrupted by the hand changing the shed, with subsequent loss of speed.

Filling a boat shuttle Use a bobbin winder to make the quill from a piece of firm paper cut a little shorter than the centre pin (Fig. 8.2). Roll the paper on to the shaft of the winder and catch the end of the yarn in the last turn of the paper (Fig.

Fig. 8.1 Spoolrack, heddle in heddle clamp, threading and reed hook, G-clamp (right)

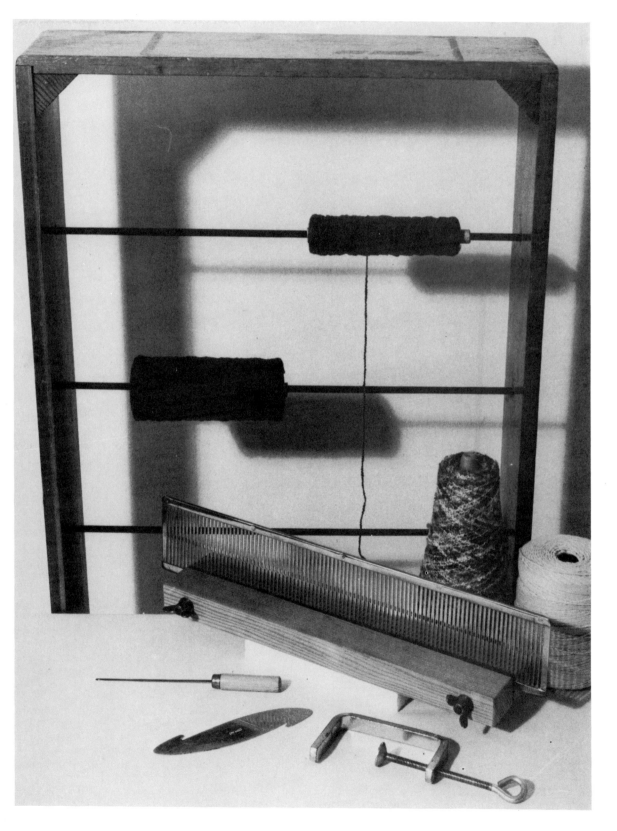

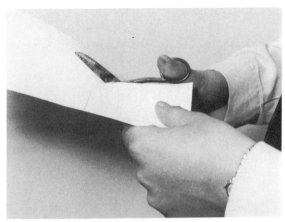

Fig. 8.2　Cutting the paper quill

Fig. 8.3　Starting to wind, securing the end

Fig. 8.4　Shaping the bobbin

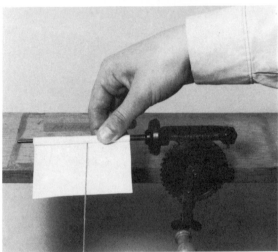

8.3). The yarn should not be wound to the edge of the paper. Wind a few turns by hand then use the winder. Build up a small mound of yarn at each end (Fig. 8.4) and then fill in the middle until it makes a firm shape, still small enough to rotate easily on the spindle inside the shuttle (Fig. 8.5). Place the bobbin in the shuttle so that the yarn runs from underneath through the hole (Fig. 8.6). Wind several bobbins at a time as the yarn is soon used up and it is annoying to have to stop to rewind bobbins.

Fig. 8.5　Finishing the shape (below)

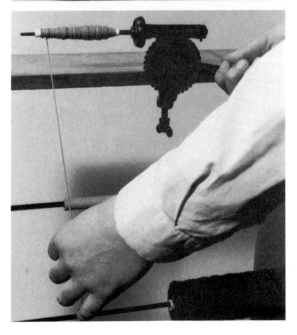

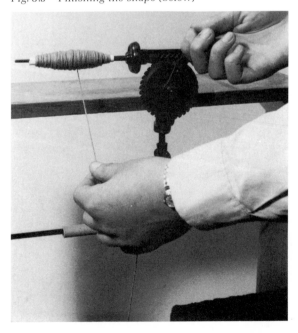

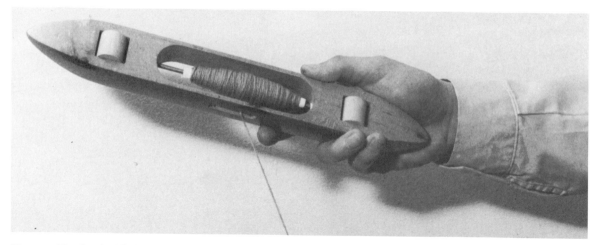

Fig. 8.6   The finished bobbin

Using the roller shuttle   Build up experience by using an empty shuttle, practising throwing and catching. Insert the tip of the shuttle into the open shed, then propel it to the other side with a flick of the wrist (Fig. 8.7). Catch it with the other hand at the opposite edge and return it. The bobbin is stopped rotating by the thumb.

THREADING HOOKS
These are essential, the main one needed being the threading hook which is similar to a crochet hook. The flat metal hook is used to thread the reed (Fig. 8.1).

Fig. 8.7   Using a roller shuttle

CROSS STICKS AND WARP STICKS
Cross sticks are flat, smooth sticks with a hole drilled in each end. They are used to keep the cross on the warp in order for threading. Warp sticks are narrower, flat smooth sticks used between the layers of warp on the back roller when winding on, and for commencing to weave to give a firm base on which to beat. Both sets of sticks are supplied with the loom (Fig. 10.1).

RADDLE
This is a comb-like device used to spread the warp to the correct width on the back beam (Fig.

15.8). It is essential when rolling on through a raddle. They can be homemade by putting nails into a length of wood at $\frac{1}{2}$ in (1·3 cm) intervals.

HEDDLE CLAMP

This is useful but not essential. It consists of two blocks of wood between which the heddle is clamped by wing nuts to hold it still while the warp is being threaded. They can be homemade (Fig. 8.1).

SPOOL RACK

This is a useful item as it holds the spools of yarn in the correct horizontal position so that they will unwind as they rotate. However, spools can be slung on string between two chairs. They can be homemade (Fig. 8.1).

HEDDLE

A rigid heddle is always supplied with the loom. Wire heddles for use with a shafted loom are also supplied with it. You may, however, feel the need to have some extra ones in addition for finer set warps (Fig. 8.1).

STRING HEDDLES

These are very useful to tie on to the shafts when a mistake has to be corrected. They can be homemade but heddle string will be needed to make them.

BOBBIN WINDER

This is essential if you are using roller shuttles (Fig. 8.4).

9
Making a warp on warping posts

Your first long warp will be made in the simplest possible manner on warping posts.

PLANNING A WARP
A few calculations are needed before you can begin to make the warp. The length, the number of threads there must be in the warp, and how much wastage must be allowed for.

The length of the warp It is always surprising the first time a beginner makes a warp to find how long a length is required to make quite a short piece of cloth. This is because of the wastage. Tying the warp to the front of the loom and the length of warp at the back which cannot be woven account for 18 in (45·5 cm) on a table loom. The take-up of the warp threads as they bend around the wefts has to be considered as well. Ten per cent of the length will cover this in normal cloth, but for finger manipulated gauze where the threads twist round each other, and honeycomb (waffle), where the deep textured surface is made up of indented cells, a more generous allowance for take-up is needed. Using wool there has to be an extra few inches to allow for shrinkage when the finished cloth is washed.

Make your first long warp in cotton, 2/6s is a suitable weight for a sampler in which you can try some of the techniques described in the chapter on plain weave. It is going to be made in one long continuous loop on a set of warping posts and then transferred to the loom. It is necessary to know the length so that the posts may be clamped along the table edge the correct distance apart.

Make it 30 in (76 cm) and add ten per cent for take-up and 18 in (45·5 cm) for loom waste. This is 51 in (130 cm), so clamp your posts to the table so that there is 51 in (130 cm) between the single and the outside double post. A heavy-duty G-clamp is recommended. It is surprising how much strength there is in yarn stretched taut between the posts.

The width of the warp and the number of threads needed to make that width Having decided how long your warp is going to be, you must now decide how many threads there should be in it. Warp threads are known as 'ends'. The number of ends in a warp depends on the number of holes and spaces there are to a unit of measurement in the rigid heddle—usually 12 or 13 to 1 in (10 per 2 cm). With the cotton chosen, 2/6s, to place one end in each hole and space will be correct. Count up on the heddle the number of holes and spaces to give the width you want. Allow an extra 1 in (2·5 cm) for shrinkage in the weaving, and double the end warp strand at each edge. Try to start and finish in a hole as this will give the neatest edge. Finished width required is 10 in (25·5 cm). To this add 1 in (2·5 cm) for shrinkage. This multiplied by the number of holes and spaces to the inch, 13, comes to 143, add two extra for double selvage. The number of threads or ends, in your first warp is 145.

MAKING THE WARP
The aim in making the warp is to place the threads in their correct order to facilitate threading the loom. Good tension of the warp and therefore a good foundation for the cloth begins with the first thread of warp that you wind. The most common fault is winding the threads too tightly on the posts so that they bend inwards with the tension of the warp strands on them. Wind smoothly and try to complete the warp in one session so that the rhythmic pulling out of the yarn and the winding is not interrupted. If you are using yarn from a cone, stand the cone on the

floor and the yarn will unwind from the top. A spool of yarn unwinds as the spool revolves so it must be supported in some way. A string through the tube in the centre slung between two chairs will solve this problem. A spool rack, if available, does the same thing.

A counting tie will be made on the long loop of the warp as it is easier to count in a series of small numbers than to keep a tally of the whole warp as it is made. The counting tie will enclose small groups of ten ends, an easy number to count.

The warp will consist of one continuous loop of threads crossing each other in a figure of eight between the posts set together in a block (Figs. 9.1, 9.3). The reason for the cross is to keep each thread in its correct sequence as you arrange them in making the warp. This order will be maintained throughout until the warp is securely threaded on to the loom ready for weaving. If you have ever found yourself in a chaotic mess trying to wind a comparatively short skein of wool you will appreciate why the cross is necessary. It is not just an invention of weavers, to make things complicated, it is the logical way of working.

Begin by tying the yarn securely to post A (Fig. 9.2). Take the thread behind post B to the front of C and round it, across to the front of B and back again to A. From A to C is one end of the warp. From A to C and back to A is two warp ends (Fig. 9.3).

Fig. 9.1   *The cross in a simple warp*

Fig. 9.2   *Tying on to start warping*

MAKING THE COUNTING TIE

After the first ten ends have been made, push a length of thick contrasting coloured yarn under the first warp thread. Take the ends of the yarn and cross them over each other to enclose the first ten threads of the warp. When the second ten has been warped, cross the counting tie ends over each other again. In this way each small unit of ten threads is held, ready for counting (Fig. 15.2).

Continue in this way until the warp is finished. As the number is uneven you will finish at the double post C. Tie the last warp back round the post and to itself.

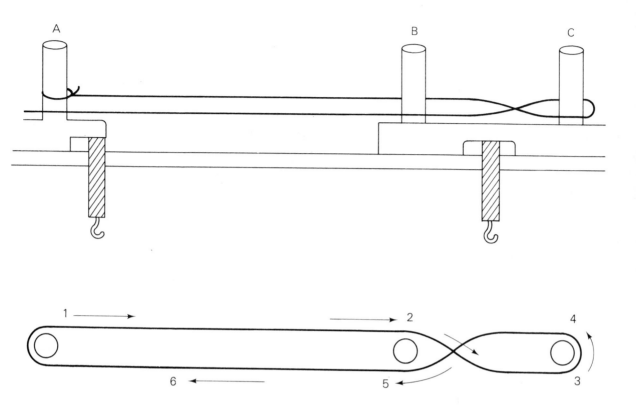

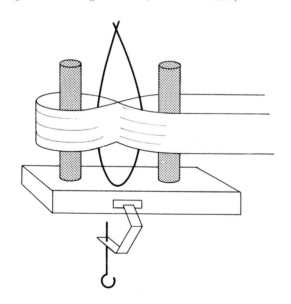

Fig. 9.3   Securing the cross (above and below)

USING MORE THAN ONE COLOUR IN A WARP

Join in the new colour with a knot as near to the post as possible. No joins must occur in the length of warp. Any knots in the warp yarn should be broken and treated as a join.

The cross must be tied up so that it will remain keeping the warp threads in their correct sequence. To do this pass a long length of thick yarn right through the two loops at the cross and knot the two ends firmly together. Another way is to put the two cross sticks in position, one in each loop at the cross, and tie them together. To make the tie joining the sticks together follow the photographs (Fig. 10.7, stages 1 and 2). Push the two sticks fairly close together with the holes opposite one another. Pass each end of a thin piece of strong string down through these holes. Bring one end of the string to the inside, and the other to the outside of the length of string between the holes and tie them with a double knot so that the sticks are parallel to each other and about a finger's width apart.

10

Weaving on a simple loom with a rigid heddle

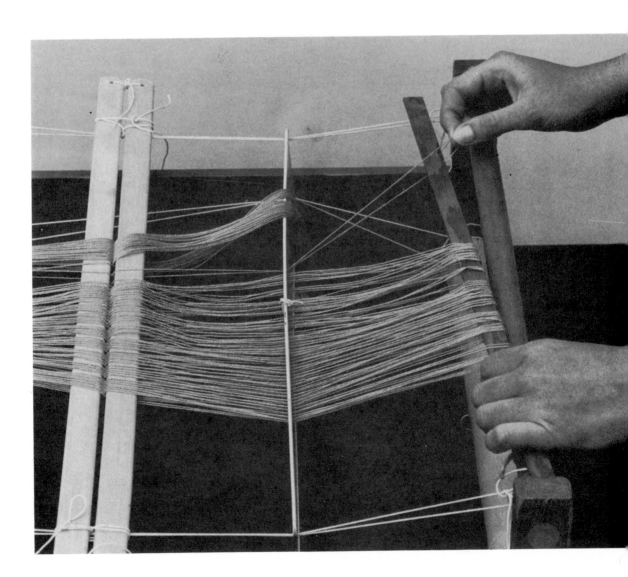

Fig. 10.1 *The pair of warp ends has been temporarily threaded through a space and is being slipped on to the loose end of a warp stick tied at the other end to the front top bar of the loom*

PUTTING THE WARP ON THE LOOM

Slip the warp from the posts and place it flat on a table with the cross towards you.

SPREADING THE WARP BY A TEMPORARY THREADING OF THE HEDDLE

At the moment the warp is in a bunch of threads as it came from the warping posts; it must be spread out on a stick to occupy the same width as it will when it is threaded ready for weaving. This will be easier to do if the heddle is held still for threading.

USING A HEDDLE CLAMP

Mark the middle of the heddle and put it between the two blocks of wood in the clamp. Tighten the wing nuts to hold it (Fig. 8.1). Place it on the table between you and the cross end of the warp. Without disturbing the threads, stretch out the long loop of the warp across the table, securing the end to a chair back. If the table is highly polished, weight the length with a heavy object.

Start from the middle so that the warp will be centred properly and, using a threading hook, pull each loop of warp from the short loop through a space in the heddle. As the loops are pulled through slip them on to a stick. Study the order of warp ends in the cross and pick up the threads in that order, one under, and the next one over, the cross stick nearer to you in a pair. When both halves of the warp have been threaded the stick on which the loops have been slipped is ready to be tied to the back of the loom.

USING A LOOM WITH SIDE SUPPORTS

Tie the heddle in position on the side supports and thread the loops through towards the back of the loom so that they will be on the stick in the right position for tying on.

USING A ROLLER LOOM WITH THE HEDDLE TIED TO THE FRAME

Place the loom on the table with the tension screw at the left, the back will be towards you. Pass two strings at each side through the end space in the heddle. Tie one to the top front and back bars, the other to the bottom front and back rollers. Rest the cross sticks on the strings tying them to the top one at each side (Fig. 10.1). Proceed to thread, slipping the loops of warp on to a stick tied to the back top bar at one side, the right side when you are threading the loops at the left-hand side, the left when you are threading the loops at the right-hand side.

When all the loops are threaded on the stick it is ready for the next stage, tying on to the back of the loom.

TYING THE WARP TO THE BACK OF THE LOOM

If the loom is new you will need string ties on the back of it before you can tie on the warp. There will be a stout piece of cloth, the apron, attached to both the back and front. A series of holes with eyelets in the apron are where the string is placed. Cut a 12 in (30·5 cm) length of firm, fine string, fold it in half and pass the loop through the hole and the ends through the loop (Fig. 10.2). Place the loom on the table with the screws controlling the tension to the left, the back of the loom is now towards you. Take the two ends of the string tie over the stick on which the warp ends are placed, bring one end up either side of the double string (Fig. 10.3, stage 1) from the apron and tie with a double knot (Fig. 10.3, stage 2). Leave a finger's width between the stick holding the warps and the stick which is in the seam of the apron. Make sure that these two are parallel. Start at each side and complete all ties.

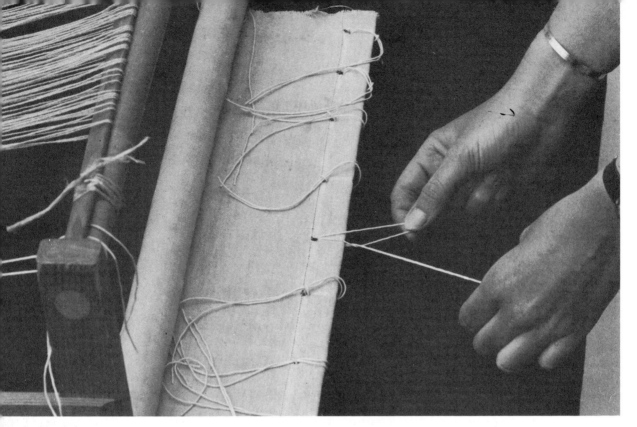

Fig. 10.2   Putting the strings on to the back apron (above)

Fig. 10.3   Tying the stick to the back of the loom, stages 1 and 2 (below)

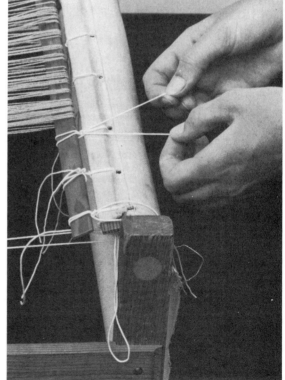

Fig. 10.4   *Beaming, rolling on (above)*

Fig. 10.5   *Rolling on alone, note paper being rolled on to back beam between layers of warp (below)*

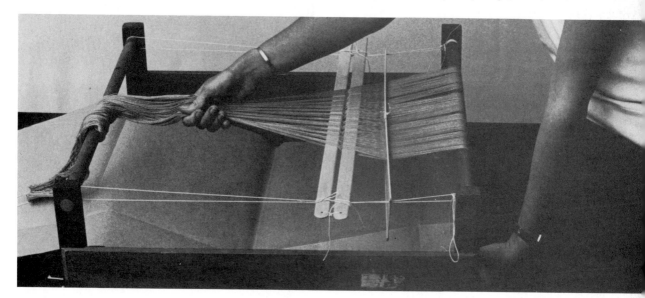

During the beaming the heddle can stay, in its clamp, tied on to the side supports or slung with string to the back and front bars. In the latter case, the string holding the heddle from the bottom rollers must be undone, to allow the roller to turn properly. The heddle need not be taken off the string until the threading is completed and the warp is ready to be tied to the front.

BEAMING (WINDING THE WARP ON THE BACK BEAM)

The back of the warp is now tied to the loom but its length must be wound on to the back beam over the top back bar. Loosen the thumb screw at the back. Beaming is best done by two people, one

holding out the warp at the front, a good distance from the loom, while the other winds it smoothly on to the back beam (Fig. 10.4). After one complete turn of warp has been taken round the back beam, secure the tension screw at the back and pull on the warp to tighten it; this should take care of any loose ends. If the warp is not too wide, this can be done alone, holding the warp with one hand and winding the roller with the other (Fig. 10.5). A shake from time to time should be all that is needed. The heddle will control the spread of the warp and each thread, with this method, is passed through the cross between the sticks.

Aim at a firm back beam with the layers of

Fig. 10.6   Transferring the cross, stages 1 and 2

Fig. 10.7   Tying the cross sticks together, stages 1 and 2

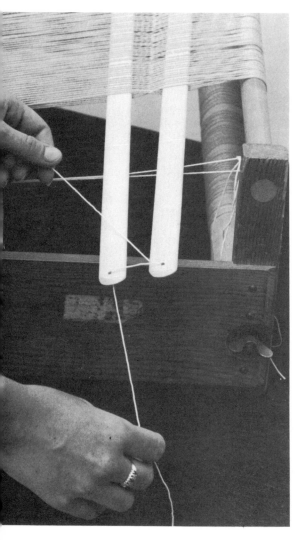

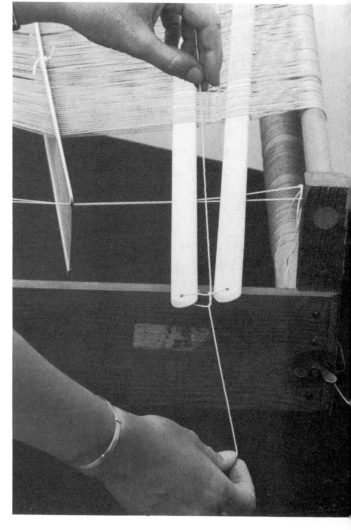

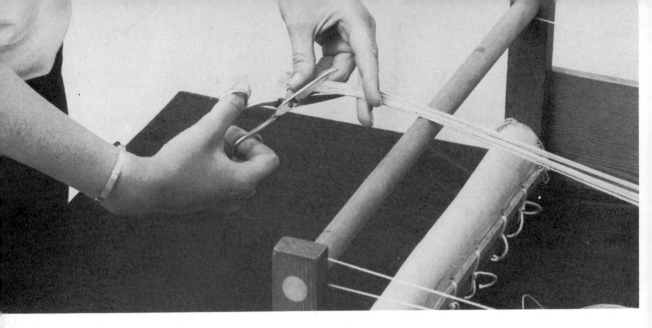

warp evenly spread (Fig. 10.5). To help achieve this, interleave the layers of warp on the back beam with sheets of firm paper (not newspaper which is too soft), or a series of warp sticks. The paper should be wider than the back beam so that the warp will not slip off the ends of each side. It also smooths out any lumps caused by the knots where the warp is tied to the back roller.

TRANSFERRING THE CROSS FROM THE FRONT TO THE BACK OF THE HEDDLE

Now the cross in the warp has to be transferred to the back of the heddle. To do this, hold the warp out taut at the front, turn the cross stick nearer to the heddle on its edge and flat against the heddle. The space formed by this will run into the warp threads behind the heddle (Fig. 10.6, stage 1). Slip a spare stick, of the same size, into this space behind the heddle, turning it on its side also. Still holding the warp taut, cut the string holding the cross sticks together, pull out the cross stick nearer to the heddle and place it in the space behind the heddle occupied by the spare stick, which can now be withdrawn (Fig. 10.6, stage 2). This has transferred half of the cross. Repeat the process with the second cross stick and finally tie them together in their correct position (Fig. 10.7, stages 1 and 2).

THREADING THE RIGID HEDDLE

Cut through the loops so that the warp ends are single (Fig. 10.8). Look at the order in which the warps come from the cross sticks. Half come over the back cross stick and under the front one. Tie these together in overhand knots to stop them slipping from their position in the spaces of the heddle (Fig. 10.9, stages 1 and 2). The other threads paired with them, which come under the back cross stick and over the front one, can be

Fig. 10.8   Cutting the warp loops

tied together in groups as well to keep them tidy (Fig. 10.10). They must now be slipped out of the spaces and replaced in the holes. Draw each one in turn out of its temporary threading in the space and rethread in the hole (Fig. 10.11). You will find this easier to do if the warp end is held taut between the first two fingers of the left hand. With the hook upwards, pull on the taut part of the thread and bring it through the hole. When completed there should be a warp in every hole and space across the heddle and double threads in the edges. Take the heddle from the block or untie it from the loom. Hold out the front of the warp and check the threading by raising the heddle to form a shed so that it is taut and so that any mistakes can easily be detected.

TYING ON TO THE FRONT OF THE LOOM

Loosen the front tensioning device and roll the apron under the front roller until the warp stick in the seam is just over the top bar at the front of the loom. Tighten the tension. Tie on a warp stick, the same size as the one inside the front apron using the knot described in the back tie up. Tie the warp to this stick. Take the middle 1 in (2·5 cm) of warp first and pull the threads towards you over the stick you have just tied down between the two sticks. Divide it into to equal parts underneath bringing each half up again at the sides and tying across the bunch of threads (Fig. 10.12, stage 1). Tension the single knot by pulling on the ends of the threads and, keeping that tension, make a second knot on top of the first (Fig. 10.12, stage 2). Test that the tension is the same by running the fingers across all the bunches.

Fig. 10.9 Making on overhand knot, stages 1 and 2 (above)

Fig. 10.10 The threads tied in groups of two layers, half in their correct positions, the spaces (below)

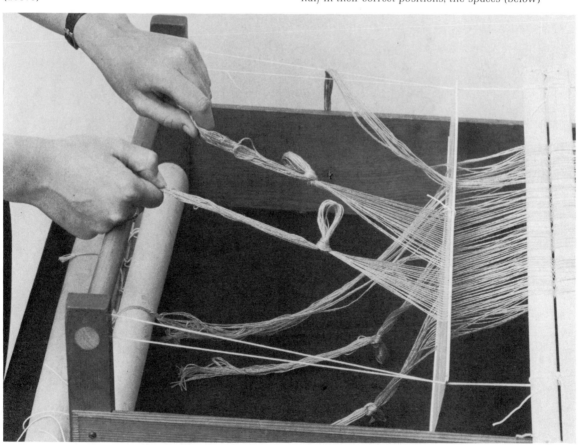

Fig. 10.11   Threading the holes (above)

Fig. 10.12   Tying on to the front of the loom, stages 1 and 2 (below and right)

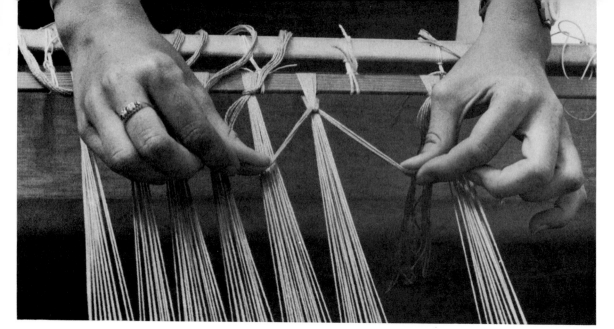

STARTING TO WEAVE WITH A RIGID HEDDLE ON A SIMPLE LOOM

Start by lowering the heddle and inserting a spare shed stick into the triangular space formed where the two layers separate. Raise the heddle to form the countershed and insert a second shed stick. These two sticks inserted in the sheds will draw the threads together and fill up the spaces between the groups of warps tied to the front.

Fill a flat shuttle, which should be a little longer than the width of the warp. Use a cotton of the same thickness as the warp. Secure the end of the weft on the shuttle by winding a few strands across the shuttle to begin with, then wind from notch to notch.

Weaving is done by raising the heddle and then lowering it to form the two sheds. Before starting to weave make sure that there is enough yarn unwound from the shuttle to weave the row. Pass the shuttle through the shed formed by depressing the heddle leaving a tail of yarn at the beginning sticking out from the shed. Bring this short length of yarn round the end warp thread and lay it with the weft in the shed. Bring the heddle towards you and use it to beat the weft into position against the second shed stick which you put in at the beginning. The first row or pick of weaving will have a double thickness for 1 in (2·5 cm) at the edge where the tail of weft has been turned in. Push the heddle back to its previous position, raising it to form the counter-shed. Pass the shuttle back through the counter-shed and beat as before. Another way of finishing off the tail end of weft from the first pick is to turn it in to the second shed with the second pick of weft after it has been beaten into place. Continue to weave in this way altering the position of the heddle and passing the weft through the shed. Try to beat evenly with the heddle held parallel to the weft and let an equal amount of warp and weft show on the surface of the cloth. Keep an even edge. Loops forming mean that you are not pulling the thread tight enough, whilst drawing in the edge too much will mean that you are pulling the weft across too tightly not allowing for the take-up on the yarn, therefore the two sides of the fabric will be pulled in instead of being straight. If the first few picks are not correct, insert a shed stick and start again with the experience of the mistakes made to help you. This first part can be undone when you take the cloth from the loom.

JOINING IN A NEW WEFT YARN

To join in a new yarn of the same colour overlap the old and new lengths of yarn between a few warp ends. This is called splicing and it can be made less noticeable by leaving the new yarn hanging out at the selvage and turning the old yarn into the next shed. After a few picks the new end may be trimmed off. When commencing to use a new colour finish off the tail of the old colour by turning it into the last pick. Introduce the new colour at the opposite selvage and turn the end back into the shed after the first pick of new colour has been woven. When a change of colour is to be used for two picks only, as often occurs in a cross check, finish off the old colour, change the shed and weave one pick right across the warp leaving an end tail of weft of 2 in (5 cm). Change the shed and turn this tail end back into it. Weave the shuttle weft across and bring it up to the top surface of the cloth so that the two ends overlap one another for a few warps. This makes a neater join. When using two colours alternately there is no need to cut and join in threads. Just carry the threads up the selvage edge. When both shuttles are out at the same selvage wrap one weft yarn round the other (Fig. 24.2).

Plain weave is the cloth that can be made on a rigid heddle but because the pattern possibilities are restricted there is no need for the weaving to be dull. All the manipulated techniques such as gauze, soumak and inlay can be tried, and tapestry is made with plain weave. The limitations in sett mean that a fairly thick yarn should be used for warp and weft but too thick a yarn is unsuitable because the threads would not pass one another satisfactorily when the heddle is raised or lowered. Grouping and spacing of warp and weft, log cabin and colour and weave effects can be experimented with.

USING A PICK-UP STICK
In addition to plain weave it is possible to use a sharpened weft stick passed under some threads to make an extra shed. The heddle is pushed down so that all the threads in the holes sink.

Working behind the heddle, pass the pick-up stick under every other end which is now up, that is the ends threaded through the spaces (Fig. 5.5). Bring the stick to the back of the heddle and turn it on its edge. This will form an additional shed in front of the heddle through which the shuttle may be passed, going under every fourth warp end across the width. A thick yarn used at intervals as an extra weft in this additional shed gives an interesting pattern called dukagång (Fig. 5.5). The pick-up stick is lodged at the back of the loom when it is not in use. A variation making a block pattern where threads pass under every fourth followed by a block in which they pass under every other thread in normal plain weave, can be made by using a second pick-up stick to make the space for the weft and then reversing the blocks.

Experiments with a pick-up stick on a colour weave effect warp can produce interesting cloth by picking up different combinations of the two colours used in the warp.

11
The four-shaft loom

Before you begin to use a loom with four shafts, study the photograph (Fig. 7.2) and identify the parts of the loom which are new to you. The warp threads will be put through the heddles according to the pattern plan, the draft, and through the reed according to the denting plan. The reed is at the front of the loom. The next few pages explain how the reed is used, how a selvage is calculated and how a pattern draft works. When you have read them you will be ready to make a more complicated warp using a warping frame, and to thread it on to the four-shaft loom.

THE REED
The reed is like a comb, made of narrow metal strips with small equidistant spaces, the dents, between them. They are always supplied with the loom, the most commonly used being eight or 14

Fig. 11.1   Paired ends in the eight e.p.i. reed

to 1 in (2·5 cm). They are available in different dents from fine to coarse and the number per inch or centimetre is usually marked on them. It is useful to have an extra reed.

The reed is held in a swinging batten at the front of the loom. It is used to separate the warp ends, keeping them parallel, to determine the sett of the warp and to beat in the weft picks. A coarse reed is more useful to have as paired ends on a coarse reed, particularly with woollens, are the usual practice in weaving rather than single denting with a finer reed (Fig. 11.1).

WARP SETT

The density of the warp in the reed—denting, setting, sleying   The way in which the ends of warp are placed in the dents of the reed is called the warp sett. The same term is used to describe the number of picks per inch or centimetre, the weft sett. The two together are the cloth sett.

There are several factors which determine the cloth sett. First, above all, the purpose for which the fabric is being made, the thickness and characteristics of the yarn, the pattern to be used and any finishing processes which will need to be undertaken.

If the warp and weft are of the same count or thickness there will be the same number of ends to picks in a set square of measurement in a balanced weave. To decide how many ends are required for this, wind the thread round a ruler for an inch or the number of centimetres marked on the reed. Let the threads touch each other without overlapping. Count the number and divide by two to give the correct dent. Plain weave is the firmest weave, there being more inter-sections of warp and weft than in any other weave, so the warp is spaced out more than for

Fig. 11.2   Crammed warp with passages of normal denting. Small pebbles inserted in the weave. Looped pile (top).

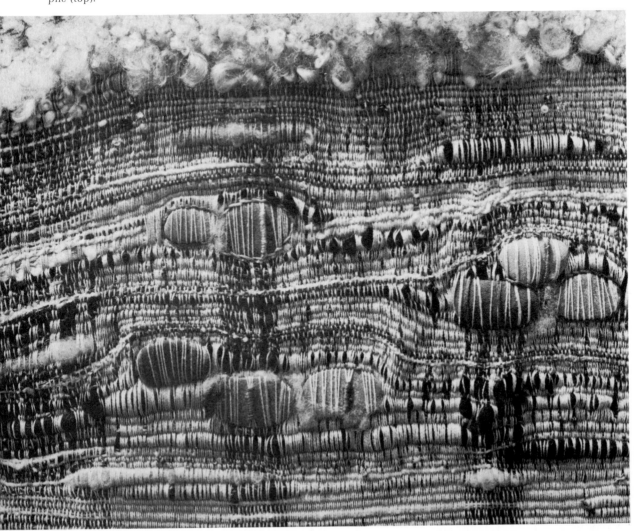

twills, where fewer intersections of yarn form the fabric. A further check on the dent is to place short ends of the chosen yarns in the reed and move them vertically past one another to see if there is enough space in the dents for the yarns to move without sticking. If it sticks reduce the number of threads in each space.

Using tweed yarn in oil, allowance must be made for washing which will make the fibres swell and fill up the spaces between the intersections. Tweed singles should be dented a little coarser to allow for this.

If the yarn counts differ, winding the warp in the arrangement to be used and testing the movement will give the overall dent to be used. With a rigid heddle the absence of a reed and the set spacing between hole and slot, limits the yarn size which can be used; too thick yarn will not make a shed. Fine yarn should be doubled unless a very lacy cloth is being designed.

Variety in density of denting can produce very interesting cloth (Figs. 11.2 and 11.3). Cramming means having more than is normal in each dent for the weight of yarn; spacing is placing less or none in each dent (Fig. 11.4). Spacing and cramming in the same warp will vary the denting used and make a variation of texture and colour in the cloth if the weft matches warp density. The warp ends are entered singly in the heddles and grouped or spaced at the reed. Keep a firm band of normal denting at each edge and limit the width and number of spaces left in the reed. A twill with the density varying in ends and picks makes a waving, curving diagonal line in the cloth.

Reeding plans which are simple can be given numerically on the drafts, e.g. reed—14× 2 means two ends in each dent (Fig. 11.5), a normal sett for 2/12s yarn and 14 dent reed (14 e.p.i.). If denting is irregular the complete plan of one

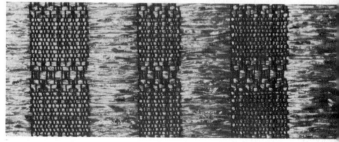

section should be given in the draft, e.g. 2/2/2/2/3/3/3/2/2/2/2/1/1/0/0/0/1/1/—29 ends in 18 dents. Abbreviated this would read—2× 4, 3× 3, 2× 4, 1× 2, 0× 3, 1× 2. The dent is shown first and the number of times it is used second. This is with a 14 e.p.i. reed.

Alternatively the dent can be added to the pattern draft as a bracket line or as a heavy line taking in the number of ends in the pattern to be entered in it. This notation can appear above the draft (Fig. 11.6).

Fig. 11.5   The warp reeded: 0,0,2,2,4,4,2,2,0,0

Fig. 11.6   The dent added to the pattern draft as a
bracket line

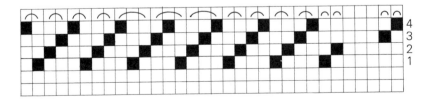

12
Selvages

A good selvage is one of the characteristics of a good piece of hand weaving but the purpose for which the cloth is intended does determine its importance. There is something very satisfying in seeing a perfect selvage form as the cloth is woven. If a cloth is destined to be cut up and sewn, however, there is little point in putting too much emphasis on the creation of an excellent selvage except as an aesthetic exercise.

The selvage is the side edge of the cloth as opposed to the fell edge which is the last pick of weaving. It is formed as the continuous weft turns round the end warp thread and returns in the next pick.

The selvage involves both the warp and weft yarn and some strengthening of the warp at the edge is necessary as it is the selvage that takes the strain of weaving. This is done on a two-way loom by doubling the end two or four warp ends, depending on the width of the warp. Using a shafted loom there are two ways of dealing with the selvage strength. Either the selvage warp thread can be doubled at the heddles and reeded the same as the rest of the warp or it can be doubled at the reed and threaded singly through the heddles. Usually it is fine hard yarn like cotton which is doubled at the reed, while softer woollens are put double through the heddles.

Selvages are threaded in twill or plain weave and the selvage must pass smoothly into the main body of the cloth without causing any fault in the web. One dent missed in the reed between the selvage and main cloth can ease out the crammed effect. Two adjacent threads must not occur on the same shaft as this would cause a fault so selvages have to be worked out for each pattern threading, extra threads may be needed to balance the pattern. The twill at the two edges of selvage threads should run opposite to one another so that, if at the right-hand edge the twill reads 4,3,2,1, at the left edge this will reverse to read 1,2,3,4.

For selvage difficulties see chapter on errors (see p. 143).

13
Pattern drafts

A woven pattern in cloth is formed by the order in which the warp ends are threaded through the heddles on the shafts, combined with the order in which the shafts are moved so that the warp and weft interlace. A pattern draft is a diagrammatic plan of a weave.

The first part, the threading plan, shows how the warp ends are entered on the shafts. Immediately underneath it follows the weave intersection plan which shows the order in which the shafts move to interlace warp and weft. The reed notation shows the denting or sleying order for the reed. Usually one repeat of the draft is enough to show the weave, but there are a few where more than one repeat must be given for clarity. Where colour has a significance, as in log cabin where two colours alternate, the colour plan should be indicated on the draft. For table looms no pedal tie-up plan is required.

Symbols for all these things vary in different countries and in different publications but the principle behind all of them is the same. Usually by understanding one system one can interpret other notations (Fig. 13.2, draft 1).

THE THREADING PLAN
Drafts are written on squared paper and occupy a number of rows of squares, the same number as there are shafts on the loom, e.g. a four-shaft loom draft will need four rows of squares to show it. Each horizontal row of squares represents a shaft and a square marked in on this row means a warp thread entered on that shaft. There are several ways of marking the squares; a filled in square, one with a line straight down through it or across the diagonal, a cross or a number (in the case of four-shaft looms, 1—4). In this book the threading and weave plans are marked with filled in squares (Fig. 13.1).

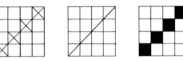

Fig. 13.1   Threading plan

The bottom row of squares represents shaft 1, the shaft nearest the reed, the second and third rows represent the middle shafts and the top row, shaft 4, the one furthest from the weaver. They are meant to look as if they are viewed from above (one way in which a pattern draft can be used to check a threading is to compare the draft with the pattern of tops of the heddles visible by looking along the shaft tops).

THE WEAVE INTERSECTION PLAN OR DRAW DOWN
This must always be shown directly below the threading plan. In the weave plan the spaces between the horizontal lines of the squared paper represent the weft picks and the spaces between the vertical lines, the warp. The crossing point where the rising warp end crosses the weft pick is shown by filling in the square. Where the weft crosses the warp the latter is hidden and this is shown as an empty square. The diagram shows the construction of the pattern (Fig. 13.2, draft 1). Complete draw downs are given for Swedish lace, waffle and a variation on rosepath (Figs. 13.2a, b and c).

When trying out a new draft, weave on paper by drawing out the draw down. This will give you some idea how the pattern is going to look.

Drafts for plain weave on a rigid heddle, or two-shafted loom, are so simple that they are seldom shown unless there is some particular colour plan in the design or an irregular sett is being used.

Fig. 13.2   Draft 1

Shaft

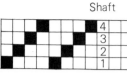

Threading plan

Straight threading 4 shafts

Weave intersection plan

Plain weave

Weave intersection plan

2/2 Hopsack

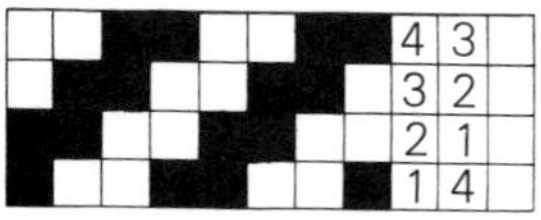

Weave intersection plan

2/2 Twill

Weave intersection plan

3/1 Twill

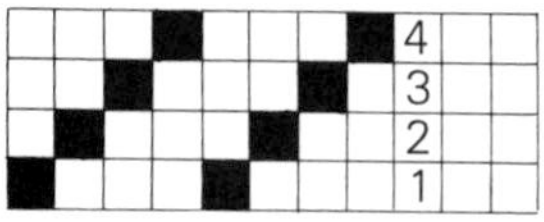

Weave intersection plan

1/3 Twill

This diagram shows the full draft for straight twill threading and the weaves possible from it. No selvages are included in the threading plan.
Shafts to be raised are shown on the right

Fig. 13.2a   Swedish lace

Threading plan

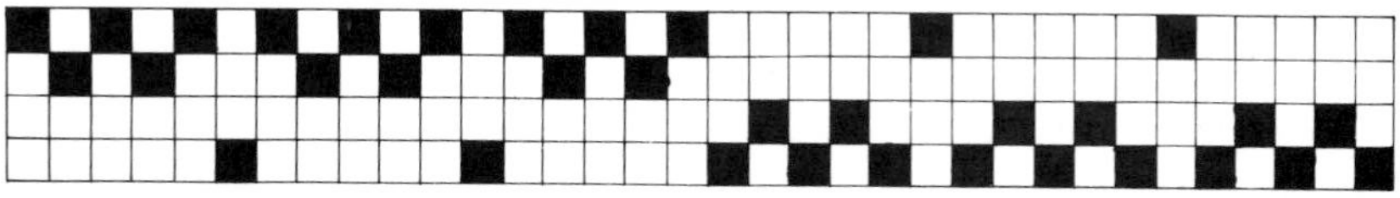

Weave intersection plan

Raise shafts: 24
123
24
123
24
13
24
123
24
123
24
13
24

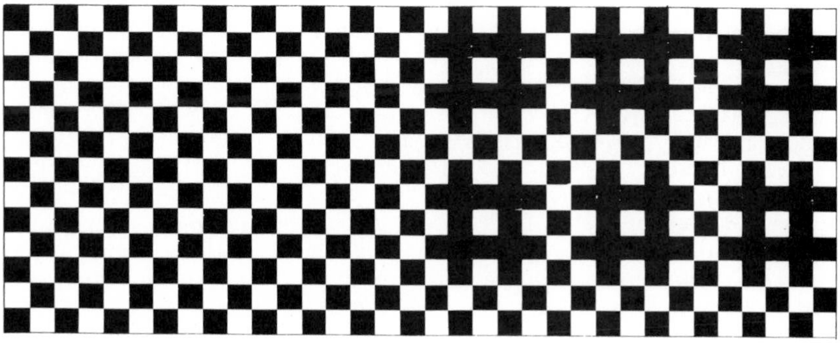

Fig. 13.2b   Four shaft waffle

Threading plan

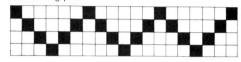

Weave intersection plan

Raise shafts:
432
431
42
3
4
3
42
43
432

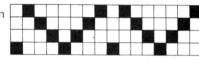

Fig. 13.2c   Rosepath

Threading plan

Raise shafts: 12
                12
Weave   41
intersection   41
plan   34
                34
                23
                23
                23
                23
                34
                34
                41
                41
                12
                12

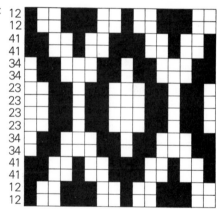

For simple threading use two rows of squared paper, the squares at the top representing the spaces or slots between the metal strips, the squares at the bottom, the holes in the strips. For the two-shafted loom, the shafts are numbered. When a square is filled in or numbered on the threading plan it means that a thread has been placed in a hole or space or on one of the two shafts (Fig. 13.3).

Fig. 13.3

The weave intersection plan is equally simple. As the heddle is pressed down, the threads in the holes are held in that position and lower with the heddle. When the heddle is raised the threads in the holes rise with it. On a two-shaft loom every other thread moves upwards when the two shafts are raised in turn. In diagrammatic terms this is a checkerboard representation of plain weave (Fig. 13.4).

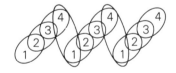

Fig. 13.4

FINDING THE THREADING PLAN FROM THE WEAVE INTERSECTION PLAN

In this book both the weave intersection order and the threading plan are given. However, if you know only the weave intersection plan you can work out the threading plan from the way the intersecting points occur, plot them and then thread the loom and weave the cloth.

Draw one repeat of the weave intersection plan on squared paper, leaving room above it so that the threading plan can be drawn in as it emerges. Start at the bottom and number the first vertical row of squares and the intersecting points on this line (1), pass to the second column and if this shows a change of intersecting points, label it (2). Pass across the whole repeat this way, taking in the whole of the plan. Where the filled in squares are the same, the numbering will be the same; it is only when a change occurs that a new number will be used. If the numbers go up to four the cloth can be made on four shafts, eight will need eight shafts.

Transfer the numbers directly above, filling them in as they occur so that they form the missing pattern threading draft (Fig. 13.5).

FINDING THE WEAVE INTERSECTION FROM THE THREADING PLAN

If you don't know the weave intersection plan you must know the order in which the shafts are to be raised in order to weave the cloth. The pattern may have been worked out for a floor loom in

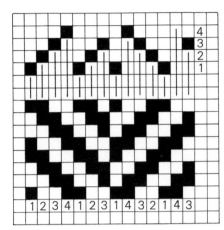

Fig. 13.5   To find the draft from the weave intersection plan

which case the pedal tie-up plan will be given. From this you can work out the shaft changes. Study one line of the draft at a time and it will show you which shafts have been connected to which pedals to produce both the plain weave and the pattern. These changes listed should make the missing weave plan.

If you know only the threading plan and have no further information, try weaving the weft with the same sequence as that of the threading plan—'woven as drawn in'. This may be the way it was intended but, if not, it may yield the key as to how to proceed.

Draw out two repeats of the threading pattern and plot the 'woven as drawn in' pattern directly below it. Circle the blocks with a ring whenever the group changes, working right across the draft (Fig. 13.6). The last thread of the last block becomes the first of the next, it is a common thread. Each small block will be woven with one less pattern pick than there are threads in the block.

Fig. 13.6   Four-shaft twill

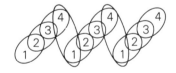

Each block woven once 2/2 Twill

ABBREVIATIONS OF DRAFTS

Long threading patterns can be abbreviated into a kind of shorthand. Instead of filling in or numbering a square to represent a thread on a shaft, a short line between the two horizontal bars will take less time to draw. Straight threading or twills can be shown as a line across the four bars, slanting the way of the twill.

14
Designing a warp for a four-shaft loom

Before you made the warp for the simple loom you had to decide how many threads were required in it. Having read the sections on warp setts, selvages and pattern drafts, you will have realized that they must be included in your calculations when you are working on a four-shaft loom. Your first warp is planned to be put on to the loom with a straight threading as this is the simplest way to start on a shafted loom. So that you will see how it is done with a more complicated draft, calculations for a point twill sampler length are given.

DETAILS FOR MAKING A WARP USING A POINT TWILL
Yarn for warp—2/6s mercerized cotton
Finished cloth—10× 28 in (25·5× 71 cm) (a sampler length)
Warp width—11 in (28 cm) (this is a rather generous allowance for take-up and shrinkage)
Warp length—48 in (122 cm) (this includes wastage and take-up allowance)
Reed dent—eight (eight threads in every $\frac{1}{2}$ in (1·3 cm) space in the raddle—16 e.p.i.)
Number of threads will be—11× 16 = 176
Number of threads in a pattern—six (29 patterns with six threads in each is 174 threads so adjust the number of threads in the warp to this as the allowance for take-up is so generous)
Allowance for twill selvage—right-hand selvage—double 4,3,2,1—eight threads
Left-hand selvage—double 1,2,3,4—eight threads
One extra thread is needed to balance the pattern (to complete the last pattern on 4). Therefore the correct number of threads will be 191 (Fig. 14.1).

The whole of the first warp using a straight threading is designed to be a sampler. You will be able to try out all the different patterns possible using the simplest draft.

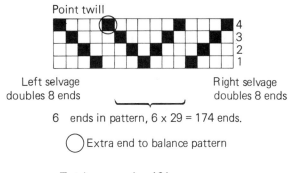

Fig. 14.1   Point twill 4 3 2 1

Point twill

4
3
2
1

Left selvage
doubles 8 ends

Right selvage
doubles 8 ends

6 ends in pattern, 6 x 29 = 174 ends.

◯ Extra end to balance pattern

Total warp ends – 191

When making future warps add some length for a sampler on which you can try out ideas. Even if you have a preconceived idea of what you want to do, experimenting first may produce a new concept. When you have allowed so much for a sampler, keep to the length otherwise you will find yourself short of warp to finish the project.

KEEPING A RECORD
Start from the beginning and keep careful records of everything that you do. Note the warp length and width, the count of yarns used, the order and sett of the warp and its total weight. Add the pattern used, the treadling order, the weft yarns used, the number of picks to 1 in (2·5 cm) and the final weight of the finished work. Include samples of yarns, the price, catalogue numbering, date of purchase and name of supplier, a small piece of cloth, before and after any finishing processes, and finally any difficulties encountered. These details will, in time, give you a valuable reference file for future projects.

15
The warp

Fig. 15.1   *Making a warp with two crosses*

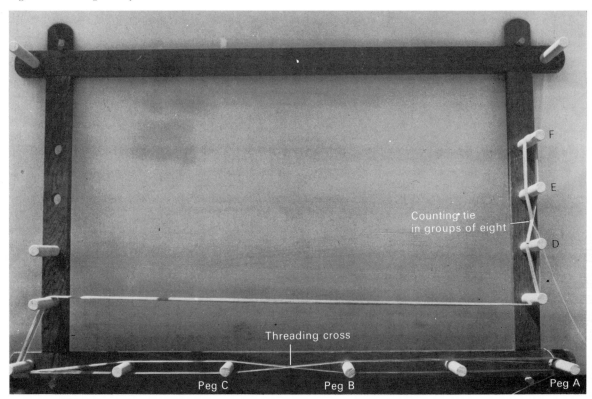

Method 1, two single crosses at each end, should be tried first. Method 2 is slightly more complicated and could be tried after experience gained using a warping board and the simpler way. In both methods the warp will then be beamed on to the loom through the raddle, the threads being passed in groups through the teeth of the raddle instead of passing through the cross as with single cross warping.

1. MAKING A WARP WITH TWO CROSSES USING A WARPING BOARD

A warping board can be used flat on a table or on a wall at a convenient height. Some pegs in it are adjustable to accommodate warps of different lengths. In longer warps the track usually zigzags across the board from side to side. Arrange the posts for the length required including loom waste, and take-up. You will need three pegs at the beginning (A,B,C) and at the end (D,E,F) of the warp where the two crosses can be made (Fig. 15.1). Before you start make sure that any peg you have moved is firmly embedded in the board.

As the warp is going to be spread using a raddle, an extra cross will be made at the end of the warp with the ends marked into groups as they will be placed in the spaces between the teeth of the raddle.

The warp of 2/6s cotton is planned to have 16 ends per inch (e.p.i.) and the raddle is divided into spaces of $\frac{1}{2}$ in (1·3 cm) between the teeth. It follows that the warps will be enclosed in a counting tie in groups of eight. Keeping a note of the groups will be easier than counting the whole warp as it is being made.

Start by tying on the thread at peg A and make a cross between pegs B and C. This is the cross you will use in threading the heddles. At the other end of the warp make a second cross in the same

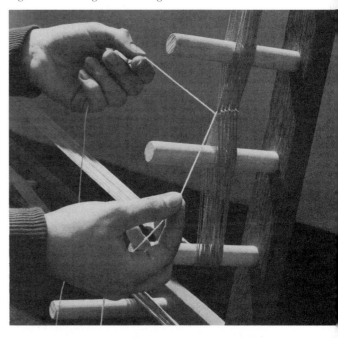

Fig. 15.2   Making the counting tie

way, marking the threads at the cross in groups of eight (Fig. 15.1). Place a length of cotton under the cross after the first eight warps have been made and cross the ends of the counting tie ready to enclose the next eight (Fig. 15.2). When the warp is completed tie the two ends of the counting tie together.

Other ties which must be made before the warp is removed from the board are ties round the two end loops at A and F and a length of string right through both sides of the threading cross at the beginning, A,B,C. The order of the threads must be preserved. If the warp is fairly long a few ties along its length will keep it tidy.

Fig. 15.3 *Chaining the warp*

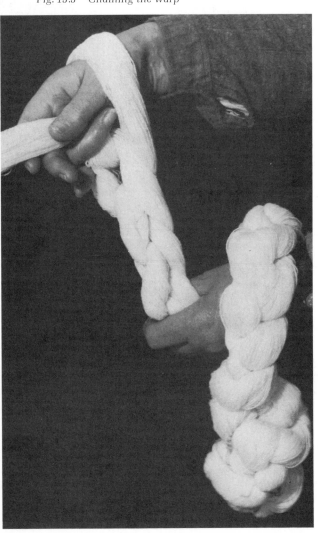

Chaining This is taking the warp off the board and looping it round itself in a crochet chain. It is the raddle cross end you will need first to tie the warp to the loom, so start the chain from the threading cross end. Pull the warp from the board and hold it taut in the left hand. Put the right hand through the loop and rest the loop on your right wrist, then grasp firmly both sides of the warp, drawing them through the loop formed like a crochet chain. Do not draw the end of the warp through the last loop or it will be difficult to start unchaining (Fig. 15.3).

2. MAKING A WARP WITH A SINGLES THREADING CROSS AND A COARSE RAD-DLING CROSS

Make a single cross between pegs B and C. Continue winding until you reach the last three pegs. There, take the first warp thread between pegs D and E, round F, where it becomes the second warp, returning it in the same track as thread one between pegs D and E (Fig. 15.4). Wind to the singles cross end and complete the second half of the singles cross in the opposite track of a figure of eight between pegs B and C. With the third thread, returning to the coarse cross end, follow the same track as the first two warps until eight threads have been warped. At the coarse cross end, take the ninth warp thread coming from peg F to the other side of peg E to start the next eight threads. When this group is completed there will be 16 warp threads in a single thread figure of eight at the beginning, B and C, and between D and E crossing in two groups of eight threads ready for raddling (Fig. 15.5).

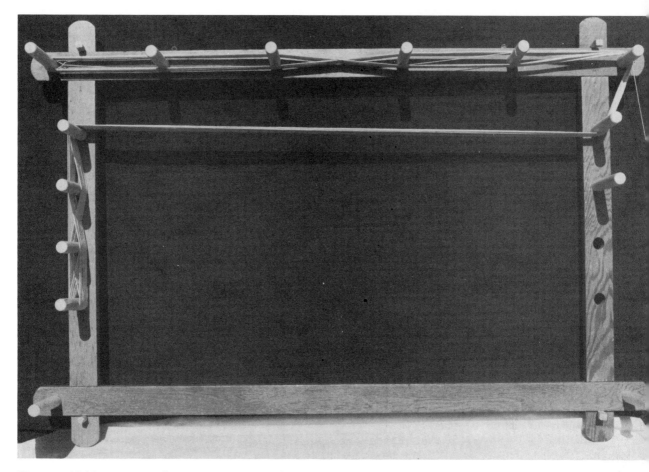

Fig. 15.4   Making a warp with two crosses, one singles
cross and one coarse cross to be used for raddling

Fig. 15.5   The coarse cross for raddling

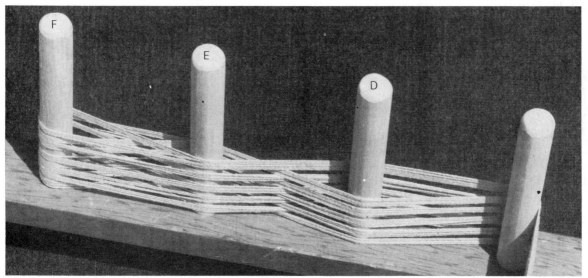

Fig. 15.6 *Looking down on the coarse cross*

Looking down on the pegs D, E and F (Fig. 15.6), the arrangement of threads can look rather confusing. *The coarse cross for raddling is between D and E.* The warps go first to one side of E for eight threads and then to the other side for eight. Loops are formed from E to turn round F. The second cross formed there is not the cross proper. Check your threads between D and E. *This is where you will tie up the cross.*

When the warping is completed, tie up as follows. Take a tie right round both of the crosses, one between B and C and the coarse cross between D and E. Tie round the loop at A and F, two ties at each side of the loops is recommended. Make some ties right round the length of the warp at intervals. Check that *all* the ties have been correctly made, particularly at the crosses, before you chain the warp. Chain as for the warp with two single crosses.

The next stage is putting the warp in the raddle so that it can be rolled on the loom.

RADDLING THE WARP WITH TWO SINGLES CROSSES

Replace the tie through the end loop at the open end of the warp with a shed stick from the back of the loom. Tying a string from each end of it across the warp is a safeguard against the loops slipping off. Starting from the centre, spread the warp by placing each group of eight threads in each space of the raddle. Complete both sides and secure the raddle top. Only·then when the warp groups are in the raddle is it wise to remove the counting tie. It can be left on; it will be rolled on with the warp. Another way is to insert two sticks into the groups of warps (Fig. 15.7).

RADDLING THE WARP WITH A SINGLES CROSS AND A COARSE RADDLING CROSS

Place the raddle on the table with the top removed and the centre marked. Replace the tie at the open end loop with a back shed stick from the loom. Tie two cross sticks through the coarse raddling cross. Starting from the middle place the groups of eight warps in the spaces in the raddle. Secure the raddle top when finished. Some weavers use a firm piece of card under the warp, as yet unspread on top of the raddle, so that the threads will not fall into the wrong space (Fig. 15.8).

BEAMING THE WARP THROUGH THE RADDLE

Tie the back stick with the warp loops on it to the back of the loom as for the simple loom. Divide the heddles, pushing them to each side of the frames to make room for the warp. If the warp is to occupy the full width of the loom, it will be necessary to remove the shafts completely. Pass the chain of warp through to the front.

As with the simple loom beaming is easier with two people. The person at the front should stand as far as is possible from the loom, walking forward as the taut warp is rolled on to the back. Both sides of a wide warp must be held out with two hands, with an occasional shake to undo the chain and even up any loose threads. The tension on the warp should ensure that the threads will be wound correctly on the back beam. With wool, where the threads tend to stick together because of its scaly construction, it may be necessary to use the hand to clear the groups as they come from the raddle. Put your fingers where the raddle teeth are. You should not split the groups (Fig. 15.9).

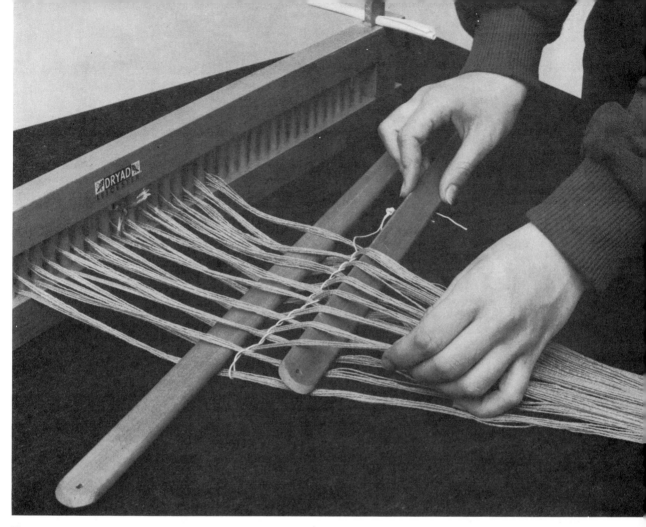

Fig. 15.7   Putting the cross sticks into the counting groups (above)

Fig. 15.8   Raddling the warp (below)

Fig. 15.9   Beaming through the raddle. Using a loom with two warp beams, the raddle is tied on to the top bar

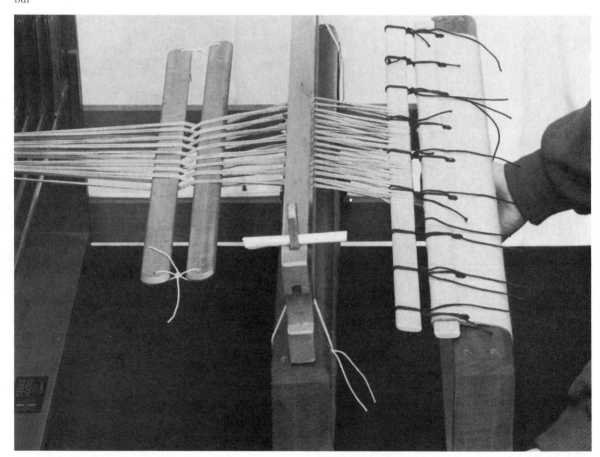

The task of the person rolling on is to turn the roller slowly and evenly, to feed in firm paper between the layers of warp and to make a firm package of warp on the back beam. Sticks can be used in place of paper.

BEAMING ALONE
As for the simple loom, work from the back and wind on a small amount at a time. After each few turns come to the front of the loom and pull steadily on the warp to tighten it more.

Fig. 15.10   The guide string in position on the mill

MAKING A WARP WITH TWO THREADS

This is a very convenient way to make a warp for log cabin weave, or to make simple warping a little quicker than warping each single thread at a time. Tie the two threads together and warp the two ends as one, remembering that when counting. They will pass together through the cross and remain double in the cross sticks. For threading take each colour in turn.

WARPING WITH A MILL

Use a guide string to determine the position of the cross bars. In Fig. 15.10, using a Harris mill, the cross bars have been placed at opposite sides of the mill for good balance. Tie the yarn to peg A. As the mill rotates the yarn will be drawn out from the cop and can be placed on the mill using the same track as the guide string and making the single and group crosses at the beginning and end (Fig. 15.11).

WARPING WITH MORE THAN TWO THREADS

Place four spools on a rack so that the thread unwinds on each spool in the same way either from above the spool or from below it. Follow the colour order of the plan; the first time you do this make the four threads of four different colours so that it is easy to keep a check on the order. Tie the threads together and on to the first peg. Draw the threads out from the rack and hold them under tension. Pass the threads under and over thumb and first finger to form a cross. Transfer this cross to the first three pegs to make the singles cross. Carry the threads round the frame or rack and make the raddle cross with the threads together in a group, keeping them in their correct order.

Fig. 15.11   Using a warping mill

16
Setting up a shafted loom

THREADING THE HEDDLES ON A SHAFTED LOOM—ENTERING

The warp, now rolled on to the back beam, is ready to be threaded through the heddles according to the pattern draft. The simplest way to thread a loom is to place a warp thread in turn on each shaft, this is called straight threading (Fig. 13.2, draft 1). Starting from the back put the first warp on 4, the second on 3, the third on 2 and the fourth on 1. If the loom had eight shafts you would start with the back shaft which would be 8, then 7, 6 and so on. The selvage ends will be threaded double.

To begin with, check that there are enough heddles on the shafts to take the warp. Count the number needed for each shaft in one pattern, repeat and multiply by the number of patterns to be threaded and add the selvage allowance. If extra heddles are needed, undo the side of the shaft and put them on. The shafts are removed, so that the extra heddles can be added, by raising them to the level of the grooves or open areas on the sides of the canopy and sliding them out carefully. Care must be taken on removing shafts, they can be damaged by rough handling. Some weavers always remove the shafts before beaming the warp, placing them on top of the canopy. With a full width this will certainly be necessary. When the heddles are correct, mark the centre points on both heddles and reed with a coloured thread and note the number of heddles on each shaft; these may not all be equal. This may save time next time. If you are not using the full width, distribute the spares equally at each side so that they do not disturb the balance of the shafts. If you are using a full width remove any extra heddles. If left, they will chafe the end warp threads and cause breaks. Check that no heddles are crossed over each other on the shafts and that

the shafts move with ease.

The threads of the warp will be entered more easily in their correct positions on the shafts if they are clearly visible from the front of the loom (where you will be threading). Push a long stick under both cross sticks tied together and rest it on the back and front bars of the loom at one side. Do the same at the other side; this will support the cross sticks firmly and the cross can be as near as possible to the back shaft for entering. As an alternative, the cross sticks can be held by a pair of string lengths tied from back to front bars at either side.

Threading can be done from one side or from the middle. The order of reading the pattern will be reversed from the middle, from right to left working towards the left, and left to right towards the right. For a beginner it is easier to start from the right side as you will learn the pattern as you enter it and to reverse the order in the middle is too confusing. Some weavers work from the centre to keep the warp in its central position and maintain the balance of shafts. It is easier to select the correct warp thread if the section of warp you are threading is under tension. Start at the right and tie the first section of warp to a G-clamp on the front bar of the loom. On a Harris loom there is a metal rod at the bottom of the batten to which the warp can be tied. Fig. 16.1 shows the warp taut under the shafts. Pick up the threads in their correct sequence as they come from the cross sticks and thread them through the eyes of the heddles on the correct shafts.

Begin by threading the selvage double. Slide the right-hand heddle on shaft 4 to the right, separating it from its fellows. Then select the first two threads from the extreme right side of the warp. Hold the two threads taut over the first

fingers of the left hand with the thumb and little finger. Then, with the right hand, hook upward through the eye of the heddle, pull on the taut part of the thread, and bring it through the eye towards the front of the loom (Fig. 16.1). Thread the next two threads on shaft 3 in the same way, the following pair on shaft 2 and the next two on 1. Working from the right, eight warp ends will have now been threaded in pairs to form the selvage.

Now begin the pattern threading singly on 4,3,2,1, taking each warp in turn as they come from the cross sequence. As each group is completed, check that it is correct and slide the heddles to the right. Make sure that the threads

Fig. 16.1   *Threading the heddles (selvages double ends)*

are not twisted round each other or the heddles, but follow smoothly from the cross sticks. As this is such a short draft, tie the warp ends in groups with an overhand knot in front of the shafts. With a longer pattern it is usual to check each pattern and tie it up. At the extreme left edge thread the last eight threads double for the selvage, reversing the order of threading so that they run 1,2,3,4. The last pattern thread must be on 2 as if it is on 1 a fault will occur in the cloth caused by threading two ends next to one another on the same shaft.

If interruptions occur when you are threading a
long draft, mark the draft clearly with a pin or
pencil mark so that you know where to continue
when you begin to thread again. Rub out the
pencil or remove the pin when you start again.
With a very short draft, e.g. twill, make a rule to
leave the work after threading 1, then you know
that you always recommence on 4.

THREADING A LONG AND COMPLICATED DRAFT

If the draft is a very long one break it down into
its block formation. Write this out with gaps
between the blocks or in columns. Each section
can be threaded and ticked off this way. Another
way to thread a long draft is to place a card
across the draft moving it along as you thread; in
that way you will always know which point of
the pattern you have reached. A pin into the draft
Sellotaped to a piece of soft board is another way.
After a time you will learn the draft.

PUTTING THE WARP ENDS THROUGH THE REED—DENTING, SLEYING

The reed is used to space the threads at a certain
distance from one another and to beat the fell
edge of the weaving. The way in which the warp
ends are threaded through will depend on the
number of small spaces, dents, there are in it and
the thickness of the warp yarn used. This will
have been decided before you made the warp.

The reed is easier to thread if it is held firmly in
one position. On Harris looms there is a locker
pin lodged in the left-hand side of the frame
which fits into a hole drilled through the side of
the frame into the swinging batten holding the
reed. On other looms tightening the tension of the
wing nut and screw attaching the batten to the
side frame at each side should hold it steady for

threading. Mark the centre of the reed and make
sure that it is resting centrally in the batten.
Release the back roller a little and pull out a little
more warp so that the warp threads can be
threaded through the reed. Spread out the heddles
if they have been pushed together after threading.

Find the middle of the warp and untie the first
bunch of threads to the left of centre. Use a fish-
shaped reed hook and draw the warps through
the dents in the reed, selecting the correct thread
with the other hand (Fig. 16.2, stages 1 and 2).
They must be taken through in the correct order
as they are threaded through the heddles; whether they are placed singly or doubled in the reed,
will depend on the plan. Make sure that the
threads are not twisted but follow smoothly from
the heddles.

Tie them into groups with an overhand knot so
that they will not slip back again. Return to the
middle and thread the other half of the warp.
Release the tension at the front and make sure
that there is a stick in the seam of the apron and
that it is just over the front bar. Tie a warp stick
of the same length to it using the same knot as at
the back of the loom. You may need to pull out
more warp from the back so that there is enough
length to tie on to the front. Use the same method
as in the simple loom and when the warp has
been tied to the front in bunches, check that the
tension is even all the way across the width.

Check that each shaft is correctly connected
with the mechanism used to raise it and that all
the shafts are level. On Harris looms this will
mean checking that each shaft is centrally slung
by its chain. For other makes you will need strong
loom cords to sling the shafts in position.

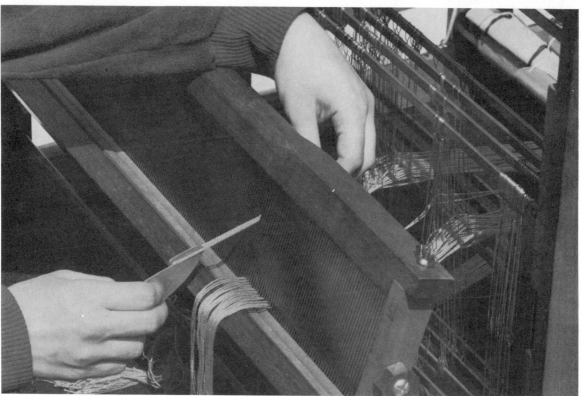

17
Using your loom

CHECKING FOR MISTAKES

Before starting to weave raise the shafts to make the sheds for plain weave in turn, 4 and 2, and then 3 and 1.

A gap in the reed is easily detected, as is an end unthreaded in the heddles, not moving with the shafts but lying in a central position. Looking through the sides of the shed you will see any thread which has been crossed between the heddles and reed. Raise the shafts for the pattern in turn. As the ends rise you will see a definite sequence of gaps across the warp width, under and over two for 2/2 twill, this also can show up a fault in the threading of the heddles which can be corrected before weaving begins. If you have checked carefully as you went along, all should be well and you will be able to begin.

WEAVING WITH A FOUR-SHAFT LOOM

The gaps between the groups of warp ends tied to the front stick will be lessened if warp sticks are used instead of yarn for the first two picks. The warp threads can be similarly drawn together by weaving with very thick yarn or rag strip for the first 1 in (2·5 cm).

Raise the shafts in turn for plain weave and insert the sticks or thick yarn. Beginning to weave the cloth after using thick yarn as a heading, insert a stick in the next plain weave shed, this will give you something firm on which to beat the picks and separate the heading from the cloth.

Use a stick shuttle, to start with. Following the pattern draft (Fig. 13.2, draft 1), weave all the possible combinations of shafts to form the various weaves. A straight entry will give you plain weave, formed by raising pairs of even and odd ends so that the individual threads interlace. 2/2 hopsack is formed by raising pairs next to one another, i.e. 4 and 3 for two picks and then raising the two shafts opposite, i.e. 1 and 2 for two picks. The different twills are made by the weft passing under the warp, moving by one end in the successive picks to make the characteristic diagonal line of the weave. Follow the diagram on Fig. 13.2, draft 1.

Plain weave (draft 1) This is formed by the shafts being raised in pairs of even and uneven, i.e. 2 and 4 and then 1 and 3.

2/2 Hopsack (draft 1) Adjacent ends are raised in pairs for two picks. Then the opposite pair are raised for two picks. It is in effect double plain weave, less strong than plain but softer to handle. Dense beating so that the wefts beat down between the warps raised in twos will make a cloth nearer to tapestry. By using 4 and 3 for several picks with a binder thread in between the picks, then 1 and 3 for several picks also, a different cloth will form with opposite blocks showing.

2/2 Twill (draft 1) This, like 2/2 hopsack, is a softer more flexible weave than plain as the intersecting points occur less frequently. Pairs of adjacent warps are raised but the progression in which subsequent threads are raised is not on opposite blocks.

The warps are raised in pairs but the threads shift by one warp each pick to form the characteristic diagonal line—4+3, 3+2, 2+1 and 1+4. Where there are the same number of ends to picks, the angle of the diagonal line will be 45°. Weaving more than one pick before the sheds are changed will reduce the angle. Twill will show most in a cloth if the twist in the yarn used for the warp is opposite to the line of the twill while the twist in the weft yarn is the same as the diagonal. Whatever the twists in the two yarns, twill will show more with passages of plain weave in between sections of twill. The direction of the twill reverses on the back.

Care must be taken with weaving the edge (see p. 144, dealing with errors).

If the order of the twill is reversed the direction of the diagonal pattern line will reverse in the cloth forming vertical zigzags. The zigzags can be small by changing direction after four picks, 4+3, 3+2, 2+1 and 1+4, 2+1, 3+2, 4+3, or larger by weaving ten or 20 picks in one direction before reversing the order. They can be woven further in one direction than the other.

3/1 Twill (draft 1)   3/1 twill is similar to 2/2 twill but is unbalanced in that the warp and weft intersect in threes and one instead of evenly in twos. It can be woven with more warp threads up and showing on the surface (3/1) or as 1/3 with more weft showing on the surface and only one warp in four raised. In each case the underside of the cloth will form the other twill, warp or weft-faced. As with 2/2 twill the direction of the line can be reversed.

All twill patterns need careful beating, there is a tendency to beat them down too heavily.

18
Pattern weaving

There are so many pattern drafts to choose from that only a small selection can appear in any general book. These have been chosen to meet different needs. Some are functional, suitable for clothing, or upholstery where hardwearing qualities are looked for; others are more decorative. It is fascinating to see the design forming in the cloth, pick by pick, along the warp. By using the drafts, some easy and others more complicated, you will begin to realize the underlying structure and begin to experiment, inventing your own patterns.

PLAIN WEAVE IN PATTERN DRAFTS
Plain weave can be woven with most drafts, the exceptions being patterns like herringbone where the ends will rise together in pairs, as odd and even ends do not alternate across the threading. On most drafts plain weave is obtained by raising 1 and 3, and then 2 and 4.

As well as being used as a border or stripe in between areas of strong pattern, plain weave picks are inserted between pattern rows on overshot drafts; they form a firm cloth underneath the floats which are a characteristic of these decorative cloths. The plain picks are called binder threads. When using a binder always use 2 and 4 shafts raised when the shuttle is entering the shed at the right side, 1 and 3 at the left. Mark the front of the loom canopy with Sellotape to start with. You will never be in doubt as to which plain pick comes next.

TWILL WEAVES
You have already had experience of this weave on your first piece of work on a shafted loom.

TARTANS AND DISTRICT CHECKS
Tartans are cloths woven in 2/2 twill in which two or more colours intersect in lines and squares (Fig. 18.1). Their charm lies in the mixture of pure and blended colour for although there may be only a few colours used, probably six or less, the number of colour combinations possible is large.

In Scotland the tartan setts had been used for centuries before they began to be known in England. They served as an armorial system to identify the families, the clans. Within some clans there were different setts; the chieftain and his immediate family had the right to a distinctive tartan; there were different setts for hunting and for formal dress.

Originally the colours used were natural dye-stuffs and there was a variety of shades using the plants of the district.

With the defeat of the Jacobites in 1746, the wearing of the tartan was banned and the clan system of family loyalty came to an end. But the cloth setts survived, based on the old pattern sticks on which were wound the threads to be used in the checks. Queen Victoria made tartan a fashionable cloth and it was then that the brilliant colouring we associate with tartans began to be used following the advent of synthetic dyes.

Today there are hundreds of cloths commercially produced in tartan setts. As well as the clan tartans, there are the Regimental tartans of which the best known is probably the Black Watch (Fig. 18.2, draft 8), with its subtle dark blend of blue, green and black. The royal family have their own. Royal and Hunting Stuart are two of the most consistently popular cloths. The various setts have been identified and analyzed so that the hand weaver can use them.

District checks are not as brightly coloured as

Fig. 18.1   2/2 twill in red, green and yellow

shepherd's plaid (Fig. 18.2, draft 5), economy was the start of the traditional pattern using the natural colours of two fleeces, black and white. Dogtooth check is set in units of four threads, warp and weft, while shepherd's plaid is in units of six. Gun club (Fig. 18.2, draft 4), crosses threads of white, tan and brown. Glen Urquhart (Fig. 18.2, draft 6), has blocks of two and then four ends crossing one another making a cloth of small and larger checks (Fig. 18.3).

When designed, both tartans and district checks should begin and end in the middle of a block.

Tartans and district checks are tedious to warp because of the frequent colour changes, but are fascinating to weave. Being woollen they are better put through a coarse reed in pairs to avoid too much wear on the threads. When weaving beat to a 45° angle, keep the shuttles in order and make sure that perfect squares appear when required in the design. Two picks of the same colour are a feature of tartan weaving. Use the method of finishing off the ends of the colour change described on page 71.

UNDULATING TWILL (Fig. 18.2, draft 7)
The line of the twill can be made to change by cramming and spacing the warp at the reed, by alternating two weights of yarn with corresponding denting across the warp or by extending the blocks of twill by threading several ends on the same shaft, using a separate heddle for each one, skipping some heddles and in this way varying the runs of twill. Make a firm edge of normal twill sett. Using textured weft yarn and varying the density of picks also, good curtaining material can be made, the design form being emphasized by the folds.

the tartans, they are formed by crossing two or more colours in arrangements of narrow stripes. In dogtooth check (Fig. 18.2, drafts 2 and 3) and

Fig. 18.2 *All patterns except undulating twill are threaded on straight threading and woven in 2/2 twill*

Tartan Setts. All genuine tartans are kept in the Tartan Register in the Scottish Tartans Society. The thread count in each colour stripe is known and if the pattern is a reversing or non reversing one.

Shaft

2 Dogtooth check

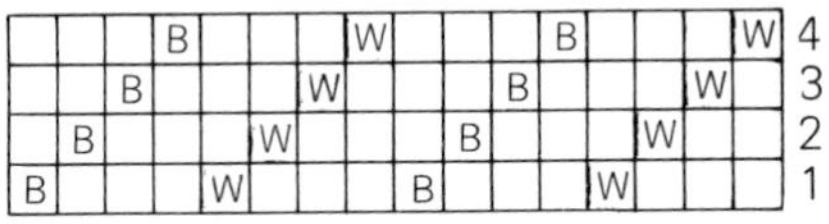

		B			W			B			W	4
	B			W			B			W		3
B			W			B			W			2
B			W			B			W			1

3 Alternative dogtooth check

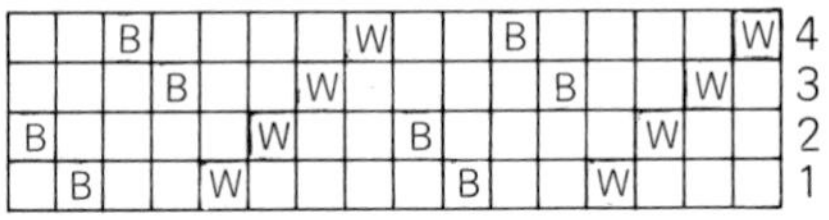

	B			W		B			W	4
	B		W			B		W		3
B			W		B			W		2
B		W			B		W			1

4 Gun club

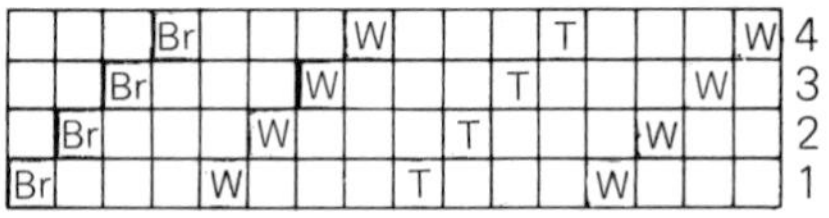

	Br			W			T			W	4
Br			W			T			W		3
Br		W			T			W			2
Br		W			T		W				1

5 Shepherd's plaid

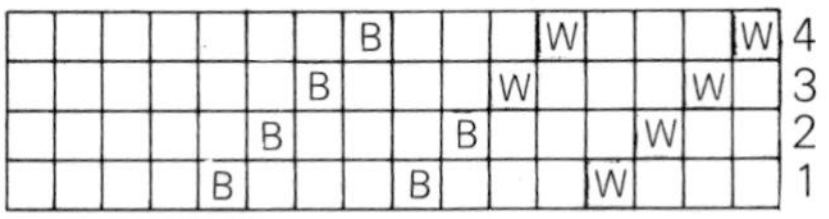

				B		W			W	4
			B		W			W		3
		B			B		W			2
	B			B		W				1

6 Glen Urquhart

Thread 12 blocks of 4 threads = 48 ends
Thread 24 blocks of 2 threads = 48 ends

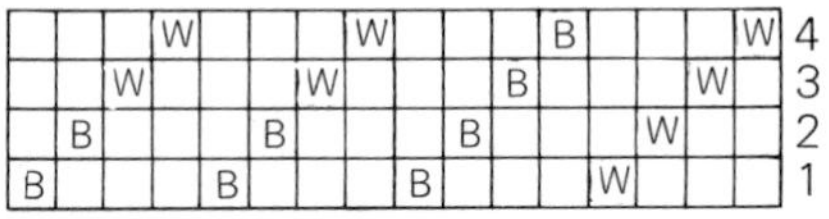

	W		W			B			W	4
W			W		B			W		3
B		B			B			W		2
B		B			B		W			1

7 Undulating twill

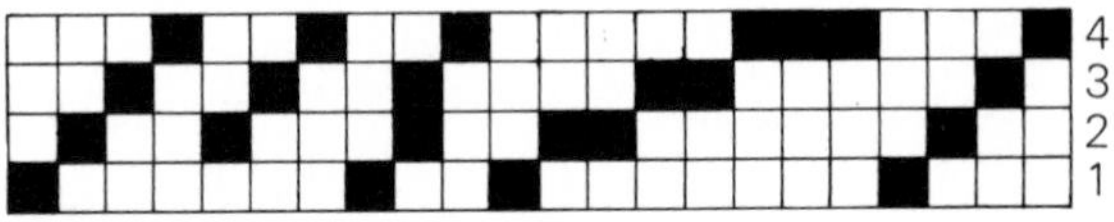

8 Black Watch.

Key to colour . . . Blue. B, Black, K, Green, G.
B 24, K 4, B 4, K 4, B 4, K 20, G 24, K 6, G 24, K 20, B 22, K 4, B 4.
This is half the sett as it is a reversing pattern.

98

Thread the encircled thread on final pattern only to balance

Shaft

9 Simple point twill

4
3
2
1

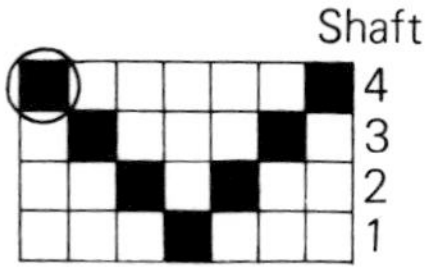

9a Treble point twill. Encircled thread on final pattern only

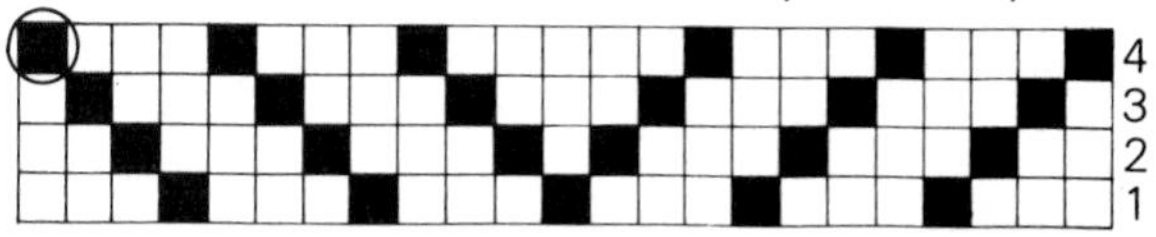

4
3
2
1

11 Bird's eye

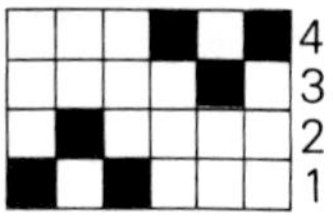

4
3
2
1

10 Goose eye

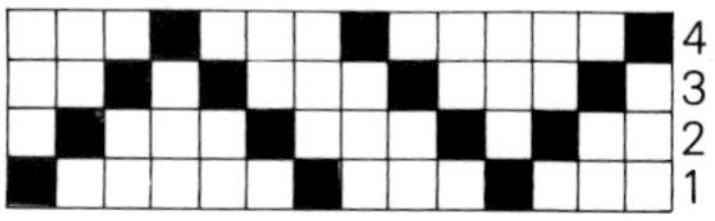

4
3
2
1

12 Herringbone

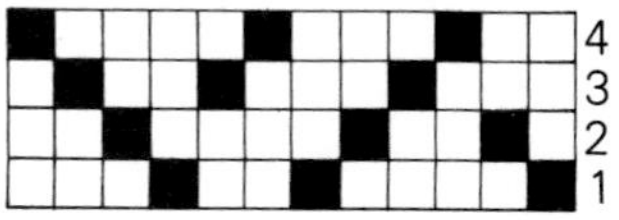

4
3
2
1

13 Rosepath

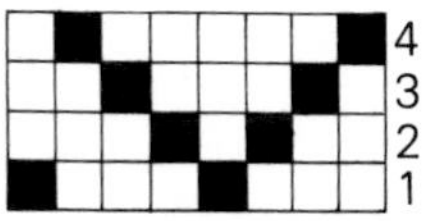

4
3
2
1

14 Undulating point twill

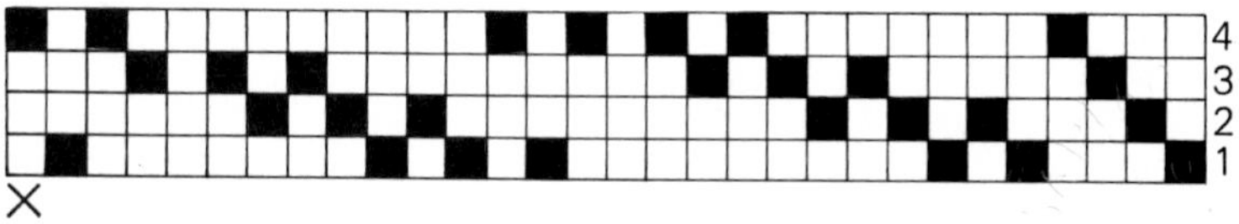

4
3
2
1

X

Centre ⟶ Reverse order back

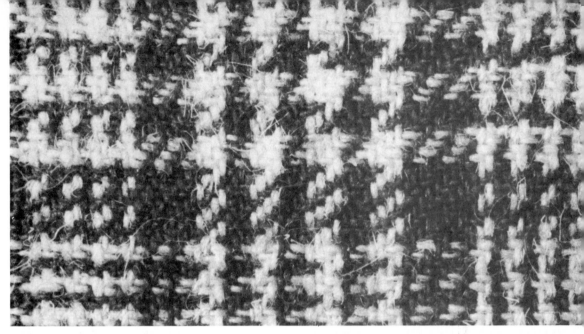

Fig. 18.3   Glen Urquhart

Fig. 18.4   Point twill reversed

SIMPLE POINT TWILL (Fig. 18.2, draft 9)

If a warp is threaded on the shafts to form a point instead of straight, the direction of the twill in the cloth changes direction also to form a horizontal herringbone from selvage to selvage. Raise shafts as for 2/2 twill. If the shedding order is reversed, diamonds will form in the cloth instead of vertical zigzags as the shape of the draft turns back on itself (Fig. 18.4). Point twills can be 2/2, 1/3 or 3/1. Raise shafts: 43, 32, 21, 14, 21, 32. Raise shafts: 4, 3, 2, 1, 2, 3 (this makes a thinner pattern line on the surface in a diamond 1/3, with 3/1 on the reversed pattern and a binder plain pick in picks with the same shafts raised in the centre of the reverse pattern and a binder plain pick in between each, an elongated diamond can be made.

Point twills can be doubled or trebled (Fig. 18.2, draft 9a). The addition of extra runs of straight twill at each side make the zigzag larger (Fig. 18.7) and when woven in reverse, the pattern forms concentric diamonds (Fig. 18.8). Raise shafts as for 2/2 twill.

For concentric diamonds:
Raise shafts: 23, 34, 14, 12, × 2 (i.e. two picks)
　　　　　　　23, 34, 14, 34,
　　　　　　　23, 12, 14, 34, × 2
　　　　　　　23, 12.

GOOSE EYE (Fig. 18.2, draft 10)

Double point twill is so-called in some books. In others the name is given to twill in which the whole threading is turned upside down. The draft reads 4, 3, 2, 1, 2, 3, 4 then 1, 2, 3, 4, 3, 2, 1. Weave as 2/2 twill for chevrons. For the goose eye, raise shafts: 23, 34, 41, 12, × 2
　　　　　　　23, 12, 14, 24, × 3.

Fig. 18.5   Point twill

Fig. 18.6   Point twill on striped warp. (The cloth has been folded to show the reverse.)

Fig. 18.7   Trebled point twill

Fig. 18.8   Trebled point twill with shedding order
reversed

Fig. 18.9   Herringbone

BIRD'S EYE (Fig. 18.2, draft 11)
This is a smaller pattern. Thread 4, 3, 4, 1, 2, 1.
Weave as standard 2/2 twill and reversed.

HERRINGBONE (Fig. 18.2, draft 12)
This is based on a point twill but because of its
structure it avoids the three thread float at the
reversal points, which makes it a stronger weave.
Weave as for 2/2 twill (Fig. 18.9) and 2/2 twill
reversed.

Fig. 18.10   Rosepath

ROSEPATH (Fig. 18.2, draft 13)
A simple and versatile weave, this is a favourite with pattern weavers. Weave as for the other drafts, as 2/2 twill to form horizontal chevrons. Diamonds are made with the following order:
Raise shafts: 12× 2, 41× 2, 34× 2, 23× 4, 34× 2, 41× 2, 12× 2 (Fig. 18.10). Use a binder. By experimenting by raising adjacent pairs many different patterns can be made.

UNDULATING POINT TWILL (Fig. 18.2, draft 14)
A point twill can be made to curve in the same way as a straight twill, by extending the number of threads on each shaft, skipping some, which interrupts the zigzags to form a stepped curve. The design form is a restless undulating shape which can be turned back on itself to enclose ovals. Raise shafts as 2/2 twill and 2/2 twill reversed. This is how overshot patterns are designed.

19
Overshot patterns

The overshot pattern is a twill derivative being made up from extensions of the blocks of threads which make twill, namely 4 and 3, 3 and 2, 2 and 1, 1 and 4. In twill the blocks consist of two threads. In overshots this has been increased to four or six threads which causes a wider area of warp threads being passed over by the weft in each block. These overshots or floats give the weaves their name. The blocks can occur on opposites as monk's belt, i.e. on shafts 4 and 3,

and then on shafts 1 and 2. They can also be formed on adjacent pairs of shafts, the last thread of one block becoming the first of the next.

Because of the floats, all overshot drafts are woven with a binder thread inserted between the pattern rows in plain weave. This makes a firm cloth underneath the decorative design. Drafts tend to be long but are not too difficult to thread if split up into smaller sections (see p. 92). Certain design motifs characterize overshots. They can be

Fig. 19.1

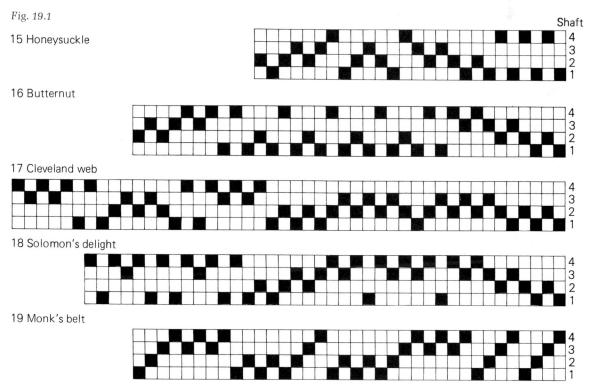

15 Honeysuckle

16 Butternut

17 Cleveland web

18 Solomon's delight

19 Monk's belt

Shaft
4
3
2
1

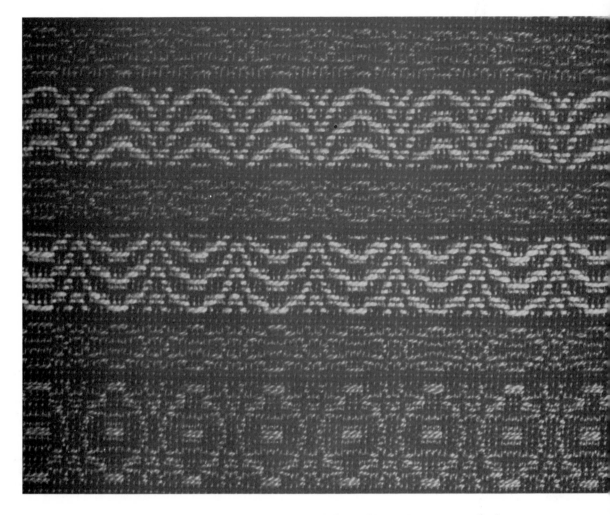

Fig. 19.2   *Honeysuckle*

woven to form shapes; a cross, rose, star, diamond, wheel and table. Combinations of these make the cloths, some being very elaborate with graceful curving lines forming enclosed shapes. They are pure magic to weave, their names as intriguing as the patterns.

The binder thread is usually the same weight and colour as the warp while the pattern thread is thicker and of a contrasting shade. A completely different use of a draft with opposite blocks like monk's belt is woven in one pale colour, binder thread finer, so that the cloth has an embossed surface.

In the overshot patterns given, no binder sheds are included in the shedding order. For those who find themselves addicted to pattern weaving, there are specialist books explaining exactly how they are formed.

HONEYSUCKLE (Fig. 19.1, draft 15)

An extra seven threads are needed to balance, threaded on 14, 14, 14, 1 (Fig. 19.2). Use a binder. Read patterns downwards in columns A, B, C etc.

Pattern 1

	Block A	Block B	Block C
Raise shafts:	23×2	12×2	14×2
	34×2	23×2	34×2
	14×2	12×2	23×3

Pattern 2

Raise shafts: 23, 34, 14, 12, 12, 14, 34, 23.

Pattern 3

Raise shafts: 14×2, 34×2, 23×2, 12×2, 14×2, 34×2, 23×2, 12×2, 14×2.

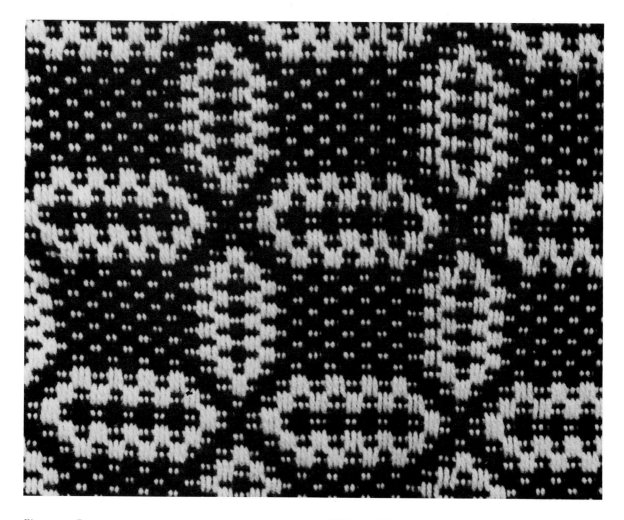

Fig. 19.3   Butternut

BUTTERNUT (Fig. 19.1, draft 16)
An extra three threads will be required to balance, threaded on 1, 2, 1 (Fig. 19.3). Use a binder.

Raise shafts:	Block A	Block B	Block C
	12× 3	12× 2	41× 3
	23× 3	41× 2	34× 3
	34× 3	12× 2	23× 3
	41× 3	41× 2	
		12× 2	
		41× 2	
		12× 2	

On last pattern add 12× 3 to square the block.

CLEVELAND WEB (Fig. 19.1, draft 17)
An extra 25 threads are needed to balance the pattern. These are threaded on the first 25 of draft, from 121 to 1 (Fig. 19.4). Use a binder.

Fig. 19.4   *Cleveland web*

	Block A	**Block B**
Raise shafts:	12 × 4	41 × 1
	23 × 6	43 × 4
	12 × 2	41 × 3
	23 × 6	12 × 1
	12 × 4	23 × 4
		12 × 1
		41 × 3
		43 × 4
		41 × 1

To see the pattern clearly it is necessary to work two complete repeats and as far as the end of first **Block A** again.

Fig. 19.5   Solomon's delight

SOLOMON'S DELIGHT (Fig. 19.1, draft 18)
An extra 27 threads are needed to balance the pattern threaded on the first part of the draft from 121 to 121. Use a binder.

	Block A	Block B
Raise shafts:	12 × 3	14 × 4
	23 × 4	43 × 2
	43 × 4	14 × 4
	14 × 2	43 × 2
	43 × 4	14 × 4
	14 × 2	
	43 × 4	
	23 × 4	
	12 × 3	

Fig. 19.5 shows a variation on the draft.

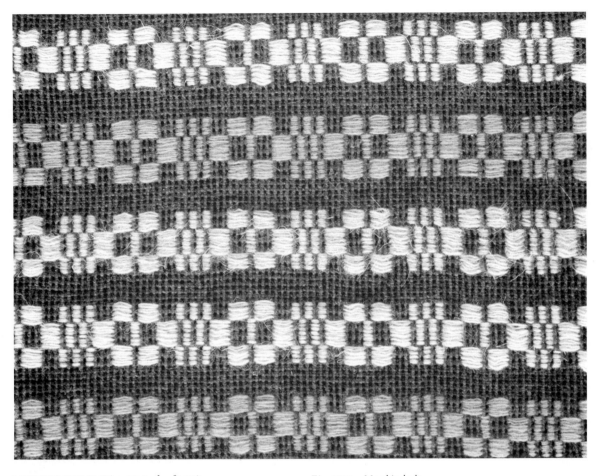

MONK'S BELT (Fig. 19.1, draft 19)

An extra eight threads are needed to balance the pattern, threaded on 4, 3, 2, 1, 4, 3, 2, 1. Use a binder.

Pattern 1—Raise shafts: 34× 2, 12× 2, 34× 2.

Pattern 2—Raise shafts: 34× 4, 12× 6, 34× 4, (Fig. 19.6)

Pattern 3—Raise shafts: 34× 2, 24× 1, 13× 1, 12× 4, 24× 1, 13× 1, 34× 2.

This is a two block pattern threaded on opposites. If the two opposite blocks are used continuously with colour changes used either regularly or irregularly, most interesting striped blocks are formed in the fabric, with small areas of plain weave in between (Fig. 19.7).

Fig. 19.6   Monk's belt

Fig. 19.7   Monk's belt, woven on opposites

20
Log cabin and colour and weave patterns

These can be woven on a simple rigid heddle loom or with four shafts and a straight twill threading.

LOG CABIN
Two colours alternate in warp and weft. End and end is used to describe the warp. Usually there is a marked difference between the contrasting pair of colours. The tonal difference between the two shows up the design well but it does not have to be in black and white. The pattern draft reads black and white, merely meaning that there is a considerable difference between the colours.

For teaching purposes, a wide range of colours of different character, but all in the same pattern, can promote discussion on the effect of colours. In a colour and weave sampler, the two chosen may be tones of the same colour or within a range of one colour which produces a dazzling contrast when used, e.g. bright pink with orange or tan, turquoise with emerald.

The warp is threaded through the heddle or on the shafts in alternating colours, in blocks, the colour order reversing at the start of the next block. This means that there are two threads of the same colour next to one another at the block change. When woven in the same two colours alternating in the same way in the weft, small motifs will form in the cloth of horizontal or vertical stripes, resembling the logs in a cabin wall. This is a simple cloth to weave which looks far more complicated that it is (Fig. 5.4).

COLOUR AND WEAVE SAMPLER ON TWO SHAFTS OR USING A RIGID HEDDLE
An extension of the log cabin and a useful way of gaining experience in the effect of colour contrast in weave, is to thread the loom with two colours only, placing the threads in different arrangements. Colour is again represented by black and

white, only some of the variations possible being used.

Divide a warp of 260 ends into ten equal blocks of 26 ends each. Then warp and thread as follows:

Block A	all black
Block B	end and end, 1 white/1 black
Block C	reverse the colour order, end and end, 1 black/1 white
Block D	2 black/2 white
Block E	2 white/1 black, finishing with 2 white
Block F	3 black/3 white, finishing with 2 black
Block G	1 black/3 white, finishing with 1 white
Block H	3 black/3 white, finishing with 2 black
Block I	2 white/3 black (start with 1 black to make a smooth run in to the last pattern)
Block J	all white

Make the warp long enough to weave the same weft pattern across in blocks to form squares. Add enough warp for experiment using other colours. When completed this can be kept in the piece or cut up and the raw edges finished off by a zigzag stitch on the sewing machine and used as a swatch of samples. Double the size and it is useable as a teaching aid to show the difference between loom state woollen cloth and properly washed cloth.

LOG CABIN ON FOUR SHAFTS (Fig. 20.1, draft 20)
Thread the shafts in black and white on every other shaft. Experiment with the different combinations of shafts. Using 1/3 twill and reversing the order gives an interesting variation.

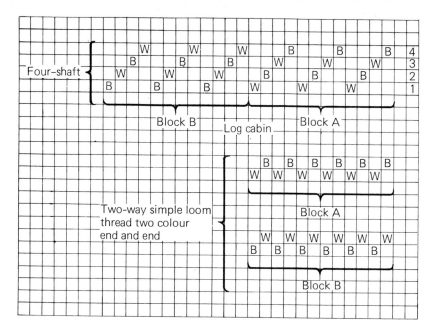

Fig. 20.1   Draft 20, log cabin

COLOUR AND WEAVE SAMPLER ON FOUR SHAFTS

The addition of pattern possibilities with four shafts widens the scope of the design. As well as some of the same arrangements of colour change used for plain weave, 4 black/4 white must be included so the change of colour occuring at 4, the start of the straight threading, and the 2/2 twill order of sheds will make a dogtoothed check in the cloth.

If the choice of colour used in a colour and weave in plain weave had a very pronounced tonal difference between the two warps, your choice this time could be of more subtle colours, nearer in tone.

With the scope of different raising of shafts many varieties of weave can be explored.

Most patterns can be woven in more than one way. Varying the order of the shaft changes will show this, one of the simplest ways being to reverse the order from a particular pick.

COLOUR AND WEAVE SAMPLER USING DIFFERENT DRAFTS

Another type of sampler warp is to use not only straight threading but some of the derivations of twill such as herringbone, goose eye, diamond or broken twill. These can be threaded in blocks with the colour of warp changing with each pattern change. All can be used with the standard order of sheds for twill. It may be necessary to change the start of some of the patterns to ensure that each one runs smoothly into the next. Design on squared paper first before making the warp. The colour choice could have strong contrast between the colours or consist of more subtle changes. As you weave keep a careful note of the threading and shed order and label the actual squares of cloth with iron-on tape when you have finished. An amazing number of cloths will emerge, some more interesting than others, some looking better on one side than the other. Often in this kind of work an accidental blend of thread and colour will give an extra bonus, providing an idea for design. The use of fancy yarns and wefts of various thicknesses and colours will all add to practical experience and leave the beginner with an understanding of design, colour, weave and behaviour of yarn.

21
More pattern drafts

SUMMER AND WINTER WEAVE (Fig. 21.1, draft 21)

This is basically a block weave and the name comes from the way in which the warp predominates on one side and the weft on the other. If one is dark and the other light, the coverlet could be used light side up in the summer and dark side up in the winter. It is a clear cut pattern and, as no thread floats over more than three warp ends, it is a suitable weave for upholstery.

Every alternate thread is entered on shafts 1 or 2. Plain weave is formed by raising 12 and 34.

The two blocks consist of Block ·A: 4241, Block B: 3231. The blocks can be repeated as you wish, colour change can be used in the blocks or they can be the same colour. Balance the distribution of the blocks.

There are many ways to weave this interesting draft. Use a plain weave binder pick on 1 and 2, or 3 and 4, between each pattern row.

Fig. 21.1

21   Summer and winter

Short draft shows block A (1323) and block ·B (1424) used four and three times. This can be repeated as many times as you wish finishing with A.

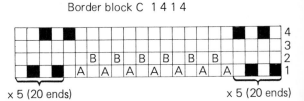

Block B   Block A

Block A 1323
Block B 1424

short draft

22   Huckaback

Thread border block five times (20 ends). Thread block A and B six times, then block A again (65 ends).

Block A 1 2 1·2 1
Block B 4 3 4 3 4
Border block C 1 4 1 4

x 5 (20 ends)   x 5 (20 ends)

23 Swedish lace

24 Canvas weave

Encircled thread on final pattern only

25 Waffle 4 shaft

26 Honeycomb

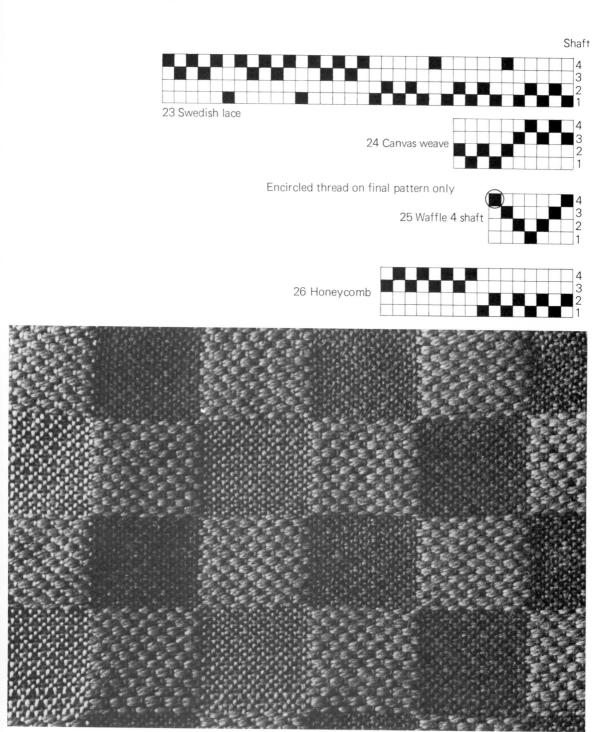

Pattern 1
Raise shafts: 13, 23, 14, 24 for four picks each.

Fig. 21.2   Summer and winter weave, woven in pairs (pattern 2).

Pattern 2
Raise shafts: 24, 14, 14, 24 and repeat to form a square.
Raise shafts: 23, 13, 13, 23 and repeat to form a square (Fig. 21.2).

Fig. 21.3   *Summer and winter weave, woven in overshot fashion (pattern 3).*

Pattern 3

Raise shafts: 24 and repeat as many times as you wish with the binder.

Raise shafts: 13 and repeat as many times as you wish with the binder (Fig. 21.3).

   The size of the blocks can vary.

Fig. 21.4   *Huckaback (linen)*

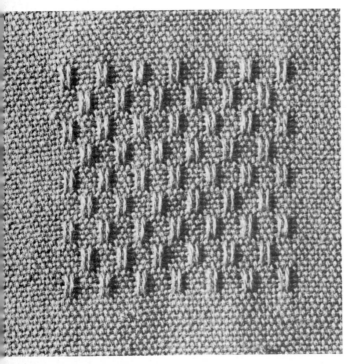

HUCKABACK (Fig. 21.1, draft 22)

In this weave, the plain weave is changed so that small floats form, the top surface shows the design in the weft, the reverse side, the design in the warp (Fig. 21.4). It is a very suitable weave for linen in one colour. The sample shown has a border in plain weave.

   Plain weave for border: Raise 42, and 31 the number of times required to form the all round border.

   In Block A the overshots are made by raising 4, in Block B by raising 1. Plain weave picks on shafts 13, accompany 4 in Block A, on shafts 24, with 1 in Block B.

Block A	**Block B**
Raise shafts 4, 31, and repeat.	Raise shafts 24, 1, and repeat add 24, then repeat Block A.

Fig. 21.5   *Swedish lace and leno lace table mat (right)*

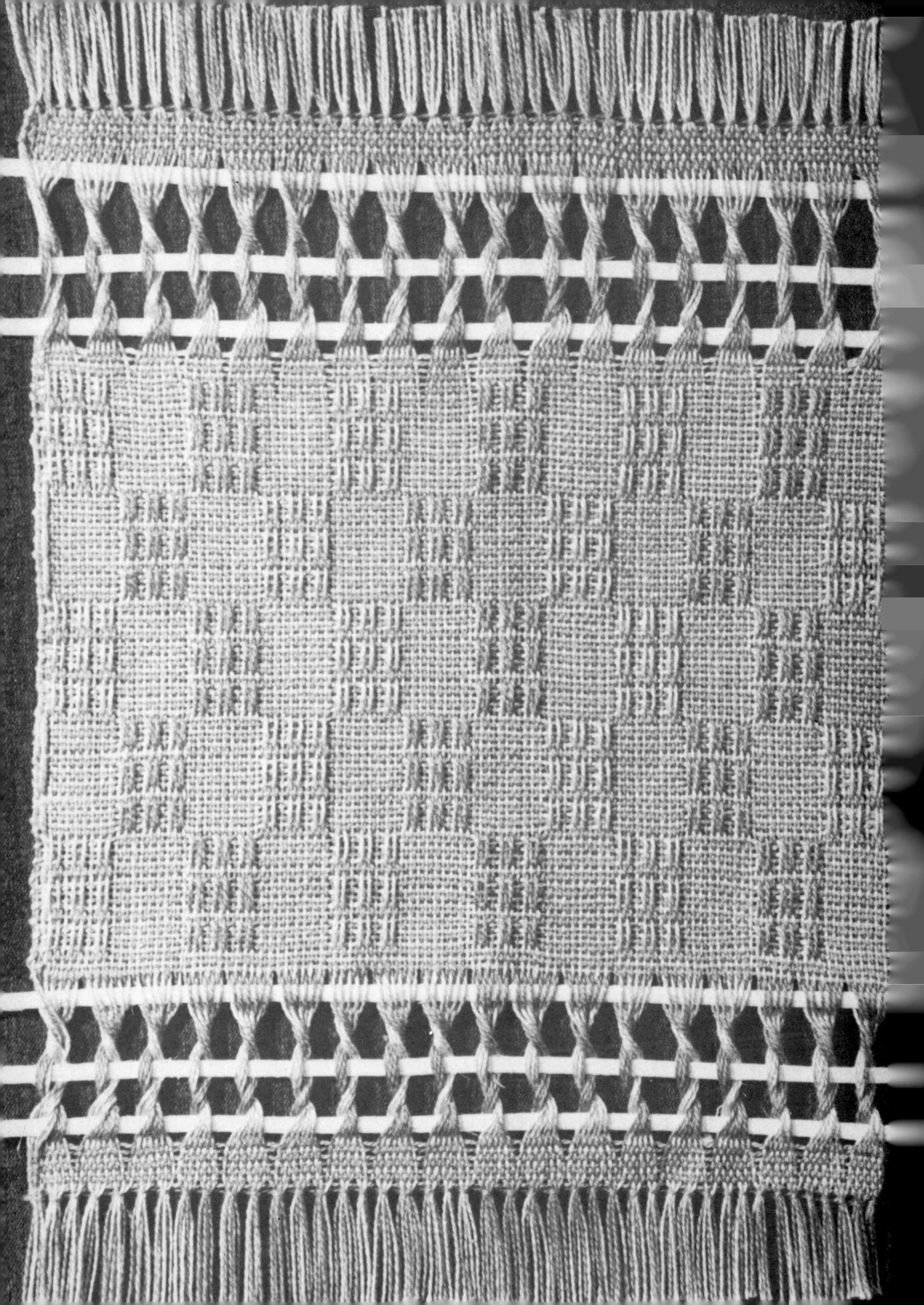

SWEDISH LACE (Fig. 21.1, draft 23)

This is a similar weave to huckaback in which small windows of lace appear in the otherwise plain weave. Loom controlled lace is not as individual or delicate as finger manipulated lace such as leno. The weave is formed in blocks, if one block is repeated the pattern will form vertical columns of lace. Swedish lace can be worked in combination with leno used in part of the fabric (Fig. 21.5). The weave can be arranged as huckaback was in the last draft to form all round borders of plain weave for table linen. Read pattern column A, then B.

Raise shafts:	Block A	Block B
	24	13
	123	234
	24	13
	123	234
	24	13
	13	24
	24	13
	123	234
	14	13
	123	234
	24	13
	13	24
	24	13
	123	234
	24	13
	123	234
	24	13

The size of blocks can vary or form squares (Fig. 21.5).

CANVAS WEAVE (Fig. 21.1, draft 24)

Another loom controlled lace. In this weave a more open cloth is made if the warp ends in each block are sleyed in the same dent in a coarse reed with empty dents at each side. Canvas can be planned with plain weave.

Raise shafts: 13, 24, for plain weave.

Raise shafts: 13, 12, 13, 12, 13,   24, 34, 24, 34, 24.

This makes an open cloth suitable for cutaining, in wool for baby blankets.

FOUR-SHAFT WAFFLE (Fig. 21.1, draft 25)

In some books you will find this weave named honeycomb. It is the same draft as a simple point twill, it is the way in which it is woven which makes it into waffle. The name describes the surface texture. Long floats of warp form at the sides of an indented square while the weft makes floats at top and bottom. The pockets of cloth inside the square are deeper with a loom with six or eight shafts but quite deep texture can be made on four.

Cross checks look well in this weave and by using two colours, one on shafts 1 and 2 and the other on 3 and 4, the squares are outlined, the reverse colour arrangement occurs on the other side of the fabric. Wool is recommended for waffle as the picks will stay in place when beaten in firmly. Extra warp allowance should be made as the weave draws in and the warp should be closely sleyed. Waffle is suitable for blankets, as the cellular structure gives extra warmth.

One extra thread is needed to add to the last pattern on 4.

Raise shafts: 432, 431, 42, 3, 4, 3, 42, 431. Finally add 432 to balance the pattern. When using two colours on shafts 12 and 34, weave picks on 3 and 4 in the same colour which has been threaded on shafts 3 and 4. This will outline the square (Fig. 21.6).

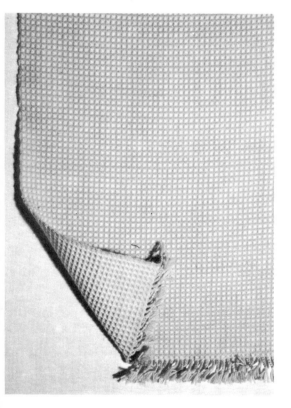

Fig. 21.6   Two-colour waffle

HONEYCOMB (Fig. 21.1, draft 26)

Honeycomb is a two block pattern in which a heavy weft forms curving lines around areas of plain weave to form oval shapes. It is a one-sided fabric as weft floats form on the reverse. The tension on the loom should be fairly loose to allow this distortion to take place. It can be woven in one colour to make an embossed surface on the fabric or with a contrasting heavy yarn to outline the shapes and enhance their colour.

Thread in eights on opposites, i.e. 2, 1, 2, 1, 2, 1, 2, 1, then 4, 3, 4, 3, 4, 3, 4, 3.

Raise shafts for plain weave 13 and 24, and weave in fine yarn the same as the warp for 16 picks.

Raise shafts: 24, and weave in a thick contrasting yarn, let the weft lie loosely in the shed and beat it in carefully. The distortion will not show when you start, only after some cloth has been woven.

Raise shafts: 134 × 4 (eight picks)
234   use fine yarn.

Then raise shafts 13, and weave in the coarse yarn.

Raise shafts: 124 × 4 (eight picks)
123   fine yarn.

Continue like this, the picks in thick yarn being woven alternately on 13, and 24.

A slight variation is to reverse the order of the heavy plain picks, i.e. 24, 13, 13, 24, in this method the distorting picks pack down over the edge of the finer yarn more closely. This is an interesting weave as there are many variations with which to experiment.

22
Double weave

DOUBLE WEAVE ON FOUR SHAFTS

Two threads are required to make plain weave so any loom on which there are four threads can be used to make double cloths. The two fabrics are made one on top of the other; they can be in two completely separate layers or joined at one or both edges. When planning for a double cloth, remember that you will need double the normal denting, half for each cloth. For clarity use two colours of a strong contrast, these are threaded singly through the heddles and double the normal denting at the reed. Colour A will be on shafts 1 and 3, colour B on shafts 2 and 4.

Selvages on double weave   If the cloth is to be two unconnected layers, make the last two or three threads *for each layer* double through the heddles.

If the cloth is to be joined at one side, make the end threads at the open side double, the side which is to be joined with single threads.

If you are making a tube, use single denting at each edge for the last two or three warps as the edges tend to tighten up.

If the cloth is to be joined at one side but is to be opened up to give double the finished width, do not thread the first warp thread in the pattern as this would cause two threads to come together down the centre making a fault in the cloth.

TO MAKE A FABRIC IN TWO SEPARATE LAYERS

Making two cloths with colour A on top   Work ten picks in plain weave.

Raise shaft 1 and weave with colour A which is threaded on shafts 1 and 3.

Raise shaft 3 and weave with colour A which is threaded on shafts 1 and 3. This has made the cloth for the top layer. So that you can weave the

lower layer, keep these two shafts up, and raise the alternate shafts to make the cloth in colour B.

Raise shafts 1 and 3, and 2 (the first shaft for second cloth), and weave in colour B.

Raise shafts 1 and 3, and 4 (the second shaft for the second cloth) and weave in colour B.
Continue like this repeating these four stages and keeping the two weft colours uncrossed at the selvage.

This will make two cloths, colour A on top, and B underneath. Now reverse the colours, bringing colour B to the top.

MAKING TWO CLOTHS WITH COLOUR B ON TOP

To give the threads room to change places, weave two extra picks on the top layer;

Raise shaft 1 and weave with colour A.

Raise shaft 3 and weave with colour A.

To start colour B on top raise the same shaft as was used last on the lower layer, namely shaft 4.

Raise shaft 4 and weave with colour B.

Raise shaft 2 and weave with colour B.

Raise 2 and 4 up out of the way and raise 1 also to weave in colour A (lower cloth this time).

Keep 2 and 4 raised, lower 1 and raise 3 and weave in colour A the second pick to make the lower cloth.
Repeat these four stages.

Practise changing layers and make a striped cloth (Fig. 22.1). These horizontal pockets can be stuffed lightly after they have been removed from the loom. Stripes of different colours can be used. Lace weaves such as leno can be made on the top layer only or groups of wefts can be wrapped. The top layer of threads can be left unwoven and the floats can be cut if desired. They should be cut with the fringe towards the reed and are best

Fig. 22.1 Four-shaft double cloth, exchanging colours

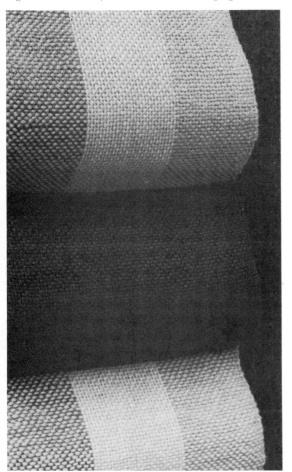

'Fig. 22.2 Double cloth fringing

done with the warp under tension. As the threads will be all from one of the two colours, A or B, they can be varied (Fig. 22.2).

TO WEAVE A TUBE JOINED AT THE SIDES

For a tube with colour A on top and B on the bottom:

Raise 1 and weave with colour A.

Raise 1 and 3 and 2 and weave with colour B.

Raise 3 and weave with colour A crossing it over colour B at the selvage to join the edge.

Raise 1 and 3 and 4 and weave with colour B.

Keep locking the wefts at the edge by crossing them.

TO WEAVE A TUBE WITH ONE COLOUR A

The method is the same as for the above, but only using one shuttle. The resultant cloth will be pure colour A on the top and a mingling of the two colours on the lower cloth.

DOUBLE CLOTH, PICK-UP DESIGN

The colours of the top and bottom cloth can be exchanged to form a design by using a pick-up stick. This is a stick with a sharpened point. Begin with a simple motif, e.g. a straight edged shape. Mark the threads where a colour change is to occur with a marking yarn (Fig. 22.3). Keep a good tension on the warp and work as near to the front beam as is possible. Use a flat shuttle as the shed formed on a rising shed loom is small.

1. Raise shafts 2 and 4 (all the ends in colour B) and slide the pick-up stick under the threads that are in the design in the first row. Shafts 2 and 4 are now relaxed and the colour B threads will remain on top of the stick. Raise shaft 1 (colour A) and make a clear shed by bringing the beater towards you and then pushing it back. Press the stick, with the colour B warps on it, back against the reed so that the threads raised can have colour A passed underneath them. Weave with colour A under the pattern, colour B warps as

well as the shaft 1 warps. Pull out the pick-up stick and beat.

2. Now raise shafts 1 and 3 (all the ends in colour A) and slide the pick-up stick under all the background threads. Drop shafts 1 and 3 and the background threads will remain on the stick, while the threads raised in stage 1 will now be under the pick-up stick. Raise shaft 2 (colour B) and make a clear shed as before. Press the pick-up stick against the reed and weave with colour B. Pull out the pick-up stick and beat.

3. Raise shafts 2 and 4 (colour B) insert the pick-up stick under the same warp ends as in stage 1. Drop shafts 2 and 4 and raise shaft 3 (colour A). Use the beater to clear the shed and press the pick-up stick back against the reed. Weave with colour A. Pull out the stick and beat.

4. Raise shafts 1 and 3 (colour A). Slide the pick-up stick under the background threads as in stage 2. Drop shafts 1 and 3. Raise shaft 4 and bring the beater towards you and back again to clear the shed. With the pick-up stick pressed against the reed, weave with colour B. Pull out the pick-up stick and beat. This is illustrated in Fig. 22.3, stages 1 to 5. If you have difficulty in passing the shuttle take out the cross sticks; they are not essential once the warp has been threaded. If the shed is still too narrow raise the back on the loom (see p. 143). A double cloth woven in rather sticky tweed wool may not be possible dented double the normal denting, as it really should be. In that case dent less closely and use a thicker weft to increase the density of the cloth. The use of a small sample before embarking on a large project is recommended. Fig. 22.4 shows cloth woven in a checkerboard using a pick-up stick in double weave.

Fig. 22.3   Stage 1, black threads on 2 and 4 raised, pick-up stick under pattern threads (above)

Stage 2, pick-up stick back against reed, picked up ends on top (below)

Stage 3, weaving in colour A (grey) (above) Stage 4, background threads on pick-up stick (below)

Stage 5, the shed has been cleared, background threads
on pick-up stick against reed—weaving in colour B
(black) (bēlow)

DOUBLE WEAVE ON EIGHT SHAFTS (Fig. 22.8, draft 28)

The additional shafts make possible block patterns, the threads being threaded either on the front or back four shafts in straight threading. Contrasting colours are recommended, threading light on evens and dark on odd shafts. As two cloths are being made simultaneously double the normal denting is required. A short draft is given, one filled in square A means four threads on 1, 2, 3, 4, block A or 5, 6, 7, 8, block B. The design of the blocks should balance.

Fig. 22.5   Two-block eight-shaft double cloth

Pattern 1   (Fig. 22.5) Weave with two shuttles. The technique of weaving is to keep up all the threads in one layer while making the two sheds for the second layer. The fabric made is very strong.

Insert the shuttles so that the dark weft weaves the dark square.

	Block A
Raise shafts:	1245
	2567
	2347
	4578

	Block B
Raise shafts:	1568
	1236
	3678
	1348

Repeat each block to square the block.

Fig. 22.4   Pick-up design, four-shaft double cloth

127

Pattern 2 3/1 Twill Weave in one contrasting yarn.

This makes a checkerboard pattern in which the direction of the twill in Block A runs in the opposite direction in Block B (Fig. 22.6).

Fig. 22.6 Two-block eight-shaft double warp and weft face twill

	Block A	**Block B**
Raise shafts:	1567	1235
	2568	1246
	3578	1347
	4678	2348

Pattern 3 (Fig. 22.7)
Weave in one colour Raise shafts:
Block A
1347,
1235,
2348,
1246. Repeat these four picks to square the block.

Raise shafts:
Block B
3578,
1567,
4678,
2568. Repeat these four picks to square the block.

DOUBLE WARP FACED TWILL
With the same threading and the shedding order as for the tartan/plain colour twill (see p. 138), a very thick closely bonded cloth can be woven. Use two colours which will blend with the two contrasting colours in the warp.

128

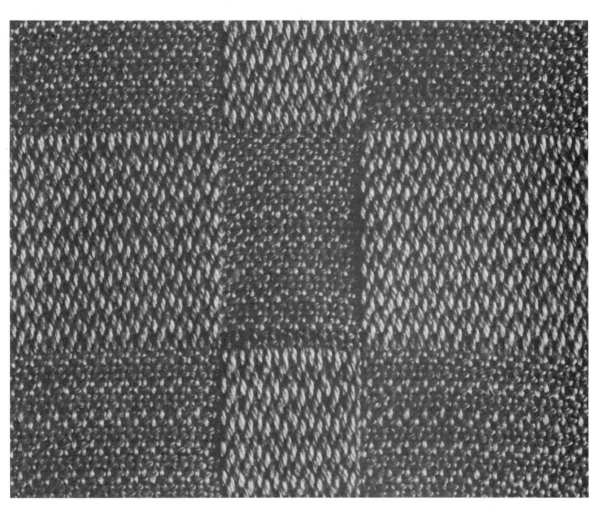

Fig. 22.7   Eight-shaft two-block (pattern 3)

DOUBLE SIDED CLOTH ON FOUR SHAFTS USING A STRAIGHT THREADING, DENTED DOUBLE THE NORMAL NUMBER

A 1/3 twill can be woven on a warp threaded in end and end on four shafts, either in the same colours or using a thicker fancy synthetic or a textured tweed.

Raise shafts: 4 colour A
431 colour B
3 colour A
432 colour B
2 colour A
321 colour B
1 colour A
421 colour B

This is not a double cloth but a double faced cloth of twice the normal thickness.

Fig. 22.8

Draft 28.

Two block , eight shaft double cloth

Short draft   A means 4 ends theaded on 1 2 3 4

B means 4 ends threaded on 5 6 7 8

Dark threads on uneven shafts 1357

Light threads on even shafts 2468

	B		B		B	B	B	B	B						B	B					B	B	B	B	B		B		B
A		A		A					A	A	A	A	A		A	A	A	A	A						A		A		A

Patterns should balance at each side.
Thread Block A BABA at edge once then B and A twice B in centre
once and reverse to start. The blocks look best kept square but
can vary in size.

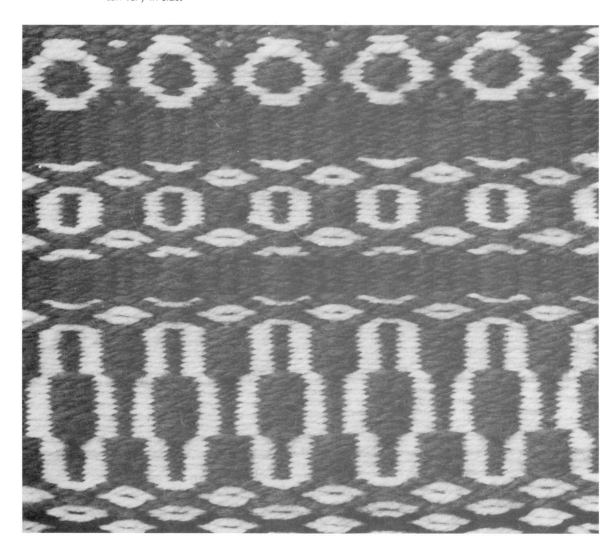

BOUND WEAVE

After each pattern pick, a background pick in the same thickness of yarn is woven on the opposite shafts. Using rosepath:

Raise shafts:			
12 colour A	34 colour A
34 colour B	12 colour B
23 colour A	14 colour A
14 colour B	23 colour B

The number of times the pattern picks are used can vary at will, each pattern pick must have its opposite woven after it. The web is like a tapestry with the colours reversing on the other side. Any of the normal shaft raisings for the pattern chosen can be used (Fig. 22.9).

Fig. 22.9 Bound weave, rosepath

23

Patterns on eight shafts

STRAIGHT TWILL (Fig. 23.1, draft 29)
As with four shafts the simplest weave is to thread straight from back to front, 8,7,6,5,4,3,2,1. Plain weave is made by raising the odd and even shafts in turn.

The structure of the twill patterns is different from that made on the four-shaft loom. It is possible to produce twills giving lines of different thicknesses showing on the cloth surface. If, for example, 2/2 twill is woven on the first four shafts, 1/3 can be woven on the back four shafts. The weave should be 2/2, 1/3 (Fig. 23.2). The weave is shown with the twill reversing.

Raise shafts: 125, 156,
                236, 267,
                347, 378,
                458, 148.

For a weave in which three different twills are woven, 1/2, 1/1, 2/1 (Fig. 23.2).
Raise shafts: 1467, 2358,
                2578, 1346,
                1368, 2457,
                1247, 3568.

For a balanced 2/2 twill:
Raise shafts: 1458,
                3478,
                2367,
                1256. Repeat this order.

For a balanced 4/4 weave (Fig. 23.4):
Raise shafts: 4321, 8765,
                8321, 7654,
                8721, 6543,
                8761, 5432. Repeat this order.

Fig. 23.1   Eight shafts

29 Straight twill

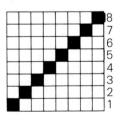

30 Using 2 contrasting colours eight ends each

31 Double sided Tartan/dark green

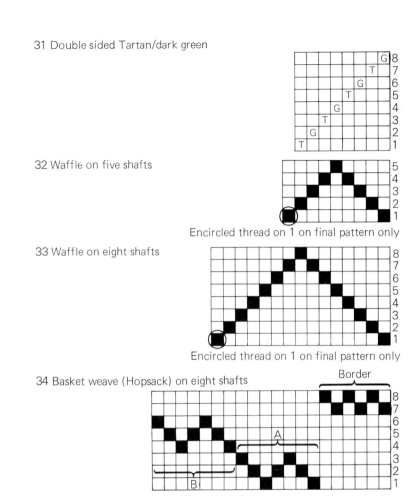

32 Waffle on five shafts

Encircled thread on 1 on final pattern only

33 Waffle on eight shafts

Encircled thread on 1 on final pattern only

34 Basket weave (Hopsack) on eight shafts

Fig. 23.2   2/2, 1/3 twill reversing

Fig. 23.3   Eight-shaft straight threading 1/2, 1/1, 2/1 twill

Fig. 23.4   Eight-shaft 4/4 twill

Fig. 23.5   Brighton honeycomb

Fig. 23.6   Straight threading in two contrasting colours, eight shafts (pattern 2)

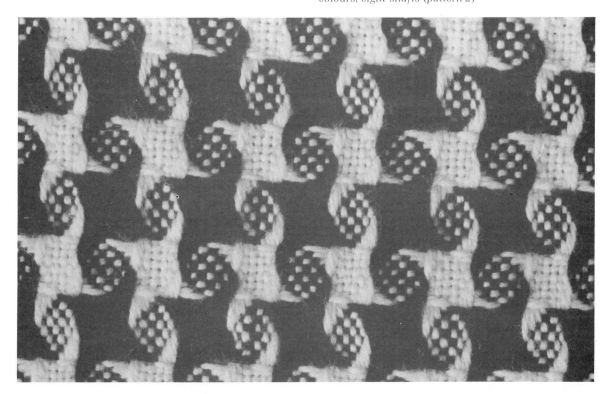

STRAIGHT THREADING USED TO MAKE BRIGHTON HONEYCOMB (Fig. 23.1, draft 29)

This is a variation on waffle (Fig. 23.5).

Raise shafts: 862,   75321,   862
731,   87642,   731,
642,

The pattern is rather more subtle than the square waffle; two sets of cells appear in the cloth. As with waffle, colour change used where the floats occur can add to the design.

STRAIGHT THREADING ON EIGHT SHAFTS USING TWO OR MORE COLOURS (Fig. 23.1, draft 30)

This can make a cloth of strong tonal contrast using black and white, or a more muted design, by using every other eight in a natural wool and alternating the other eights in pastel colours. Thread 8,7,6,5,4,3,2,1 in each colour.

Pattern 1 Raise shafts for plain weave and make a cross check using each colour in the warp in turn.

Pattern 2 (Fig. 23.6)

	Block A	**Block B**
Raise shafts:	8765,	7531,
	8764,	6421,
	8753,	5321,
	8642,	4321,

Weave the eight picks in dark and then in light colour.

Pattern 3 (Fig. 23.7)

Raise shafts:	123
	234
	345
	456
	567
	678
	567
	456
	345
	234
	123

Change yarn colour and starting at 234 repeat the sequence.

Pattern 4 (Fig. 23.8)

	Block A	**Block B**
Raise shafts:	1235	1234
	1256	2348
	1567	3478
	5678	4678

Change yarn colour and repeat both blocks in second colour.

Fig. 23.7   Straight threading in two contrasting colours, eight shafts (pattern 3)

Fig. 23.8   Straight threading in two contrasting colours, eight shafts (pattern 4)

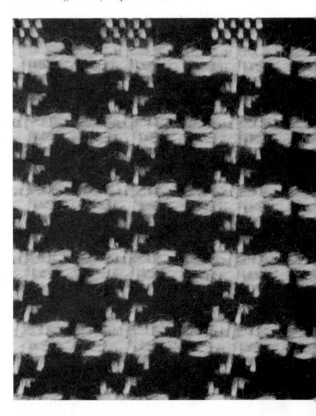

Fig. 23.9   Double-sided cloth, eight shafts, tartan/dark green (right)

136

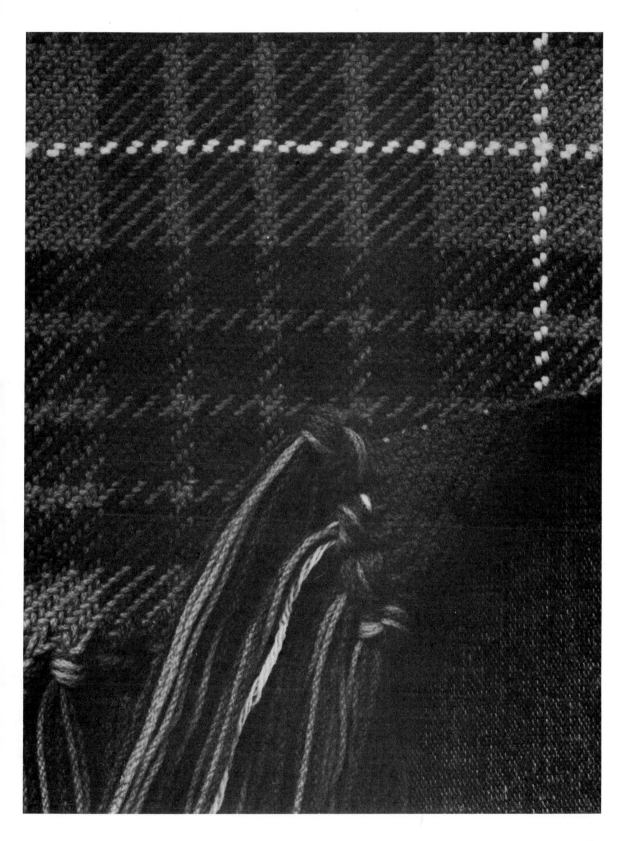

Fig. 23.10 Eight-shaft waffle

STRAIGHT THREADING ON EIGHT SHAFTS TO MAKE DOUBLE-SIDED CLOTH (Fig. 23.1, draft 30)

Colour A—shafts 1 and 3.

Colour B—shafts 2 and 4.

Raise shafts: 123, colour A

123457, colour B

345, colour A

134567, colour B

567, colour A

135678, colour B

178, colour A

123578, colour B

This weave can make good tweeds with a textured weft on the outside and a softer weft on the reverse.

STRAIGHT THREADING TO MAKE DOUBLE SIDED CLOTH, TARTAN ON ONE SIDE (Fig. 23.1, draft 31)

The tartan is threaded on the odd shafts and the plain colour on the evens. The tartan is woven on the top cloth as it is easier to follow the sett in this way. Two warp beams are useful. In the sample shown the tartan was 14 red, 2 yellow, 14 red, 8 green, 4 red, 8 green, 4 red*. Repeat from * in reverse (Fig. 23.9).

Threading using two warps Tie the two warps together, so that it is quite easy to see the lower level of plain threads. Extra care is needed in those sections of the warp where the underneath colour is the same as a passage in the tartan.

Raise the shafts: 123, tartan,

123457, plain reverse colour,

345, tartan,

134567, plain colour,

567, tartan,

135678, plain colour,

178, tartan,

123578, plain colour.

In weaving follow the plan for the tartan carefully, making sure that the wefts cross each other to give a good selvage. The two cloths will be bonded together by stitching points at intervals. Keep the shuttles for the tartan side in strict order and, when weaving passages in the tartan which are in the same colour as the reverse side, make sure that you use the correct shuttle. Mark the shuttles in some way. A different tartan can be threaded and woven on both sides.

WAFFLE ON FIVE SHAFTS (Fig. 23.1, draft 32)

Basically this is the same as on four shafts but the addition of the extra shafts makes a larger square and the pattern structure is clearer. An extra thread is needed on 1 to balance the final pattern.

Raise shafts: 1345

245

35

4

5

4

35

245

On final pattern add 1345 to balance.

As with four shafts, colour change can be used to outline the square, on shafts 4 and 5 and used as wefts when these shafts are raised alone.

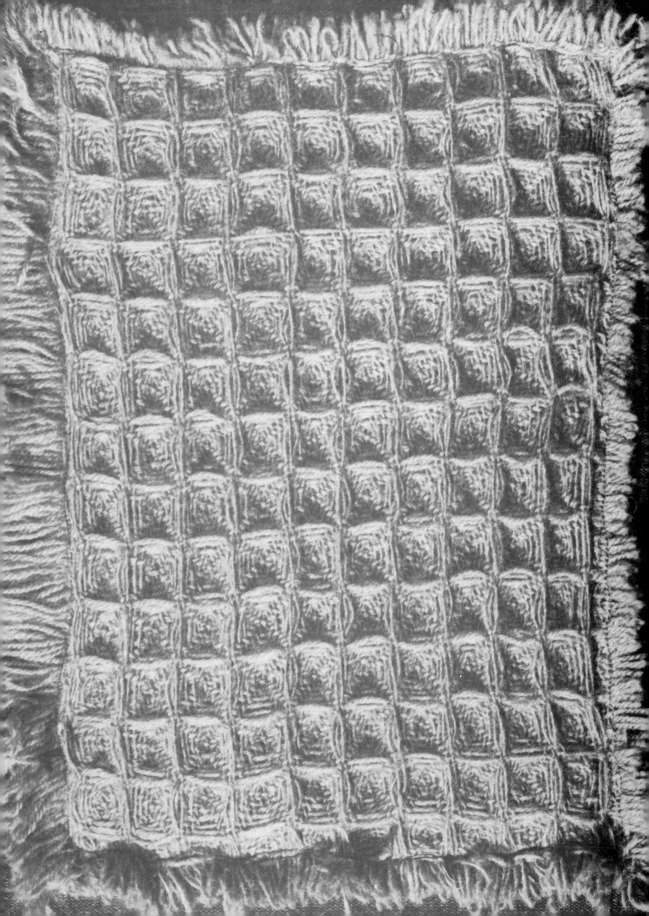

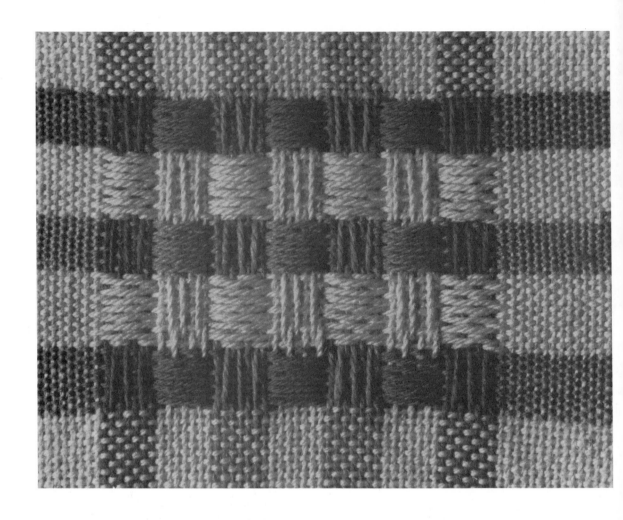

WAFFLE ON EIGHT SHAFTS (Fig. 23.1, draft 33)
This gives deeply indented cells on the cloth surface with considerable drawing in for which extra width must be allowed (Fig. 23.10).

Raise shafts:

$$\begin{cases} 1345678, \\ 245678, \\ 35678, \\ 4678, \\ 578, \\ 68, \end{cases} \begin{cases} 7, \\ 8, \\ 7, \end{cases} \begin{cases} 68, \\ 578, \\ 4678, \\ 35678, \\ 245678, \\ 1345678, \end{cases}$$

BASKET WEAVE—HOPSACK ON EIGHT SHAFTS (Fig. 23.1, draft 34)
By using eight shafts, plain weave between the pattern areas and borders can be made. This is a pattern which is best made on a loom with two warp beams as the amount of take-up between the two weaves is different, plain takes up more. The example of a baby blanket is in two colours, seven threads of colour A, seven of colour B. Finish with seven in colour A to balance the pattern (Fig. 23.11).

Fig. 23.11   *Eight-shaft basket weave*

Raise shafts: 8642, and 7531, to form plain weave, making a heading to balance the border. An extra thread will be needed on the final pattern threaded on 1 to balance.

Pattern areas

	Block A	Block B
Raise shafts:	3567,	2368
	4568,	1237,
	1457,	1248,

Weave Blocks A and B in alternating order.

Finish with Block A to balance the pattern. In the sample the blocks are repeated: A, B, A, B, A. It will be seen that as 7 and 8 rise on alternate sheds, plain weave is maintained between the blocks.

As the pattern areas must join smoothly with the plain weave borders, it may be necessary to reverse the threading order on shafts 7 and 8.

24
Dealing with errors

WARPING MISTAKES

Errors in warping can be seen and picked up when the warp is being raddled. If a stripe has been omitted, causing an uneven plaid pattern, it can be made separately as a small warp and worked in. When the warp ends are on the warp beam and rolled on after the front warp ends are cut, threads which have been incorrectly placed when the warp was made can be pulled out between the cross sticks and replaced in their correct order.

BEAMING

If the warp has not been centred properly or the tension is not tight enough it will produce a spongy back beam on which the warp has built up in places. The only remedy is to rewind the whole beam.

THREADING

Two-way loom Make a check before tying to the front by holding the warp out taut with one hand while moving the heddle up and down to make the two sheds. Any missed or double threadings will be seen.

Four-shaft loom On starting to weave you may find mistakes which must be put right at the beginning. Detect which thread is not behaving as it should and mark it with a contrasting yarn. Make sure that the thread which is not weaving in correctly is as taut as the others, it may be loose and therefore is not moving with all the others on the shafts. A very short warp end may not be held in the knot at the front. If this is so undo the bunch, join on a length of the same yarn and retie. Look through the shed sideways with the four shafts raised in turn as the error may not

be apparent on one shed but show on another. A thread may be twisted round another between the heddles and the reed and, although it may be threaded correctly, it will not be able to follow its correct track. Using string heddles it may have been threaded above or below the eye. A thread may have missed the eye completely. In that case it will remain in the middle of the shed, possibly with the empty heddle next to it. It is a simple matter to withdraw the end and enter it through the eye correctly. If, however, the heddle has been missed also, a string heddle can be tied on the shaft in the correct place.

TYING STRING HEDDLES ON TO THE SHAFT

Take a length of firm fine string, approximately twice the depth of the shaft plus 6 in (15.2 cm). Heddle twine can be bought, but any thin well twisted twine will do. Fold in half and tie with a lark's head knot to the top of the shaft where the heddle is missing. Tie an overhand or square knot level with the top of the eye and another a little below it, level with the bottom of the eye. This heddle eye must align with the other heddles. Then tie to the bottom of the shaft with the same knot used to tie the warps to the front beam.

ADDING A MISSING WARP END

If the mistake is an end missed out altogether and not wrongly threaded, it will be necessary to tie in an extra thread. Cut a length of the same yarn as long as the warp. Lay the thread over the back of the loom weighting it by tying a small object on to it. The tension should be as near as possible to the tension of the other warps. Thread it in its correct track. Thread the reed once more to the nearest selvage, a string heddle may have to be tied on.

If there is more than one mistake in a particular

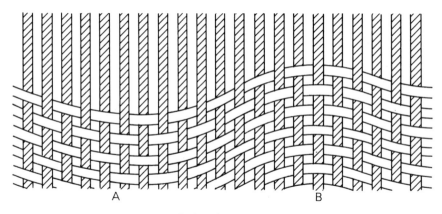

Fig. 24.1   *Warp tension uneven, slacken front warp knots at A, tighten at B*

sequence of warp there may be enough ends and heddles there, it may just be the order that is wrong. In that case it will be possible to withdraw the group and enter them once more in the correct order.

Occasionally a wire heddle may be crossed over the one next to it when it is put on the shafts. If this is not detected when threading, the only thing to do is to cut out the offending heddle with wire cutters and replace it with a string one.

HEDDLES
There is a correct top and bottom to wire heddles so that all the eyes face in the same direction as they hang from the heddle bar. When adding heddles make sure that they are put on correctly. Faults in the reed are easy to detect and re-thread to the nearest selvage.

FAULTS DUE TO THE TENSION
Check that the row or pick of weft is straight when you start to weave. This edge of the cloth, as the weaving progresses, is called the fell edge (as opposed to the selvage). Wavy instead of straight lines indicate tension faults. Look along the fell edge. Where the line of the pick rises, the tension is too slack and requires tightening. Dips downward mean that there the tension needs loosening (Fig. 24.1). If there are several errors it will be more sensible to tension the whole warp again. Check also that the sticks tied to the front are parallel to one another.

FAULTS IN BEATING
Correct beating in of the fell edge requires much practice. Using the rigid heddle grasp it in the middle or, if it is wide, use both hands, one at

each end, and beat parallel to the front of the loom. Avoid rocking the heddle from side to side as this will curve the weft. If you apply more pressure to one side, the fell edge will slope to that side. If the weft yarn is very springy it may be necessary to change the shed before beating or to beat in twice. The most common fault is to beat in too hard so that the weft covers the warp too much. There should be both warp and weft showing on normal cloth.

CORRECT BEATING ON A SHAFTED LOOM
As in the simple loom, the beater must be grasped centrally and brought forward parallel. The weight of the beater will help the uniformity of the beat but the distance between the fell edge and the reed has an effect on the pressure required to firm the pick. An even beat can only be achieved with practice. Watch carefully as each successive pick is pushed against the previously woven cloth. Take particular care when returning to weave after a break away from the loom or after moving the warp forward to tension it again. The rhythm must be re-established. Check that there are no streaks forming in the cloth as you recommence.

FAULTS IN WEAVING TECHNIQUE
Insert the shuttle near to the reed as this is where the shed is deepest. Try not to catch the tip of the shuttle on the end warp thread, this will cause breaks if done several times. Put the shuttle in with care.

Using a stick or flat shuttle, make sure that there is enough yarn unwound from the shuttle to complete the pick. Move the cloth forward frequently by releasing the back tension, letting out some warp and tensioning the front again. Working with the fell edge too near the reed means that the angle of the shed opening is too high putting undue strain on the warp ends and causing breaks. After tensioning make sure that the cross sticks are pushed back to their correct position. If they are too close to the shafts, it will cause strain and breaks. If they are resting against the back shaft, they will prevent a shed being formed.

FAILURE TO MAKE A GOOD SHED

This may be due to the way that the shafts are slung. Make sure that they are tied high up so that the shed is sufficiently deep to allow the shuttle to pass through. Make sure that chains, where they are used, are correctly linked and not twisted in any way. The fault may be that the yarn is sticky, the threads clinging together instead of dividing cleanly as the shed is made. This may clear as more cloth is made. Try increasing the tension. If this still persists the warp has been dented too close in the reed. In a rigid heddle, the warp is too thick to part properly.

In forming a shed, the upper half of the warp is put under great strain as it rises at an angle. The other half is similarly stretched when the counter-shed is formed. When using a roller shuttle, the threads at the bottom of the shed must be level with the bottom of the reed so that the shuttle can be thrown along the shuttle race. The distance between the shafts and the back of a table loom is short compared with a floor loom. This affects the angle of the shed as it is made. On some looms it may be necessary to remove the cross sticks when weaving, or even clamp a block of wood on the top back bar to raise it.

MENDING A BROKEN WARP END

It is unlikely that you will escape without any broken warp ends to mend.

Breaks will occur no matter how careful you are. Where they happen can be a help in pinpointing the cause and you may be able to stop it happening again. Breaks cannot be mended by just tying the two ends together.

Tie a length of the same warp yarn to the broken thread at the back of the loom, using a weaver's knot which is small, flat and will not slip under strain (Fig. 3.1). Follow the track of the original thread taking it through the cross sticks, heddle and reed to the front of the loom. Place a dressmaker's pin in a vertical line with the broken thread about 1 in (2·5 cm) from the fell edge, and parallel to it. Twist the end of yarn round it, winding in figure of eight fashion (Fig. 7.1). Continue to weave using the new thread. The old broken end should be left until the work is finished when it is darned in. Another way to deal with the back end of the new yarn is to hang it over the back of the loom with a suitable weight tied to it.

When the weaving has progressed so that the original warp thread is now able to be taken back into the fabric, this should be done. All ends must be darned in when the cloth is taken from the loom, before washing and finishing.

Knots in warp yarn should not have occured. They should have been picked up and dealt with when the warp was made. However, if there are knots they should be treated as a broken thread.

FAULTS AT THE SELVAGE

Keep a neat selvage without loops at the edge or drawing in of the sides. Put the weft in the shed in an arc to allow for the take-up. Hold the outside edge out between the thumb and finger of the hand not passing the shuttle.

Using two colours the yarn from one shuttle will always be over the end warp while the yarn from the other shuttle will always be under the end warp. Unless they are crossed over each other at the selvage they will not weave in properly (Fig. 24.2). With some of the weaves in which inter-sections occur in pairs, care must be taken to ensure that the end threads are included in the weave. Sometimes it is enough to start again from the other side. If not, the edge must be woven by taking the weft over or under the end warp at each side. An extra double thread not entered in the shafts but in the reed alone can be added at each side. It is moved up or down by the hand to allow the wefts to wrap round it.

Fig. 24.2 Using two weft yarns, locking them at the selvage by crossing them over each other

CUTTING OUT UNWANTED PICKS

When a colour choice is found to be wrong or actual mistakes have occurred, it will be necessary to pick back what has been done. If only a few picks are involved, weave backwards to remove them. However, if a larger area of weaving has to be picked back, it is wiser to cut out the wefts. Particularly with woollens, the interlacing of several picks will have fused the two yarns together. To separate them would cause too much roughing up of the warp, which could show when woven again and could be the cause of future breaks. Pull the warps a little away from each other and carefully insert the scissors in the small gap formed and cut out the unwanted weft threads. This should be done in several places. The weft yarn will pull out easily.

TENSIONING ONE LOOSE WARP

If a warp end works loose as the weaving progresses, it can be twisted on a pencil used like a tourniquet at the top back bar. A badly wound back beam can produce a warp which will become slack in parts. Packing soft paper between the warp and the roller may help. On a frame, individual warps becoming loose, can be tightened by a pencil twisted at the top of the frame on the offending end.

25
Finishing cloth

Fig. 25.1   Wrapped fringe

Fig. 25.2   Twisted fringe

When the cloth is woven it is cut from the loom leaving waste warp at the two ends. Any broken ends, where fresh warp ends have been substituted, must be neatly darned in. Look for mistakes on both sides of the cloth; it may be possible to cut and darn them in correctly. Trim flat any protruding weft threads.

FINISHING THE FELL EDGE

If the cloth is destined to be cut up to make a garment, it is not necessary to finish the edges, except perhaps by using a zigzag stitch on a sewing machine to preserve the edge temporarily. Machine stitching is all that is needed for samplers, they can then be mounted in a file or hung by a bulldog clip to a pinboard where they are easily available for reference.

FRINGES

Fringes are not suitable on all cloths and there are many different ways to make them (Fig. 25.1).

Hem-stitched fringe   This can be done while the cloth is still on the loom or after it has been taken off. It is the usual hem-stitch, grouping the warp threads together with an enclosing thread and a small stitch between the groups, the number in the groups depending on the size of warp threads.

Knotted fringe   Tie the warp ends with an overhand knot on the edge easing the knot close to the cloth before tightening. A more complicated fringe can be made by continuing to make knots by taking half the threads in each knot in the first row and knotting them with half the threads from the adjacent knot. This will cause the second row of knots to occur half-way between the first knots, hence the name it is given, honeycomb.

Macramé knotted fringe   Rows of horizontal cording placed close together form a very firm edge, while diagonal cording makes a lighter but more decorative edge. Groups of warps can be used as one thread to make flat knots, bannisters or chains.

Plaited fringe   Plain three-thread plaiting as used in hairdressing is the simplest kind, by using more threads in the groups making a rounder more decorative braid.

Twisted fringe   Pull out the length of warp twisting it tightly. Then double it back on itself. It will twist round itself automatically to form a firm double twisted fringe. This can be done with pairs of ends or groups. A similar twisted fringe

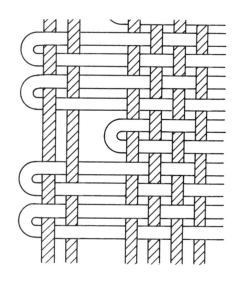

Fig. 25.3 Woven selvage fringe

can be made like this. Pull out a group of warp ends and twist them tightly in the same direction as the yarns themselves twist. Prevent this group unwinding while you are twisting the next group in the same way. Hold on to the ends of both groups and place one on top of the other. Let the ends go and the second group will go in the opposite direction, spiralling round the first. Knot the ends together to stop them unravelling. Both these twists look very effective with a two-coloured warp. They are easy and quick to make. Weight the cloth down on a table top allowing the warp strands to hang down. In this position they twist easily (Fig. 25.2).

Loop fringe This needs forward planning because you start to make the fringe when you commence weaving. Start weaving and make a heading of 2 in (5 cm). Weave in a strip of firm card twice the required width of the loops and weave the main body of the cloth. When this is completed, take it off the loom and complete the fringe by placing the edge of the cloth and the edge of the extra piece of weaving together, pulling out the card and hem-stitching the two edges together. An uncut looped fringe will form.

Woven edge The warp ends can be woven into the other ends as a weft. Take the first pair of ends at the left (the wrong side of the cloth uppermost), and weave them to the right under and over five pairs of threads, bringing them to the surface and away from you. Do the same with the next pair at the extreme left edge and continue in this way until the right edge is reached where a bunch of threads will be left. These can be made into a tassel or twisted.

Selvage fringe A fringe can be made at the sides of the cloth on the selvage. Add four extra warp ends at each side of the warp where you wish the fringe to end. Pass them through the reed only. When weaving, take four picks through at each side to the edge of the extra warps, then two picks to the selvage of the cloth only. This will fasten the edge threads and prevent them from slipping. When the weaving is finished, the extra warp threads are pulled out and the loops in the selvage fringe cut to match the fell edge fringe. This makes a continuous fringe round such articles as place mats (Fig. 25.3).

PRESSING AND WASHING

Cloth made from cotton and synthetics does not usually require any special finish except where cotton is expected to be made up into a garment, when it is washed to establish whatever shrinkage is going to take place. Pressing may be necessary, in which case it should be done on the wrong side.

Linen improves with washing and pressing and should be ironed damp on the right side as the action of a heavy iron on the yarn will flatten it and make it shine. Cotton and linen need a hot iron, synthetics a cool one.

WOOLLEN FABRICS

Woollen cloth must be washed and fulled particularly when the cloth has been made from wool in oil. The oil will be removed making the colours brighter. The fibres will swell, filling up the spaces between the weave and causing a degree of shrinkage.

Use plenty of hand hot water and soap, not detergent. If the length of cloth is too long to handle easily in a large sink use the bath. It is essential that there is adequate water around the

cloth as it must not be rubbed to remove the oil and dirt. Use several changes of water and rinse carefully in the same temperature of water. This washing process is called 'scouring'. Squeeze out surplus water.

Milling or fulling should now take place. The clean cloth is now immersed in a thick soapy solution, the minimum of water and a lot of soap, and milled by beating with the hands until the fabric feels right and the warp and weft no longer slip on each other. Walking on the cloth in the bath is the best way to full larger lengths. This will make sure that the whole length of cloth receives the same treatment. Turn the cloth regularly and watch constantly for the right degree of fulling which will vary. To go on after the correct stage has been reached will cause felting which cannot be remedied. Rinsing is an essential part of the process, and several rinses will be necessary. The wet cloth must not be wrung, surplus water should be squeezed out or removed by a light spin. Placing it between towels, flat, and changing the towels several times is a good way to get out the water with short pieces, as the cloth can remain flat.

Drying is an equally important part of the process. It must be slow, setting the cloth so that, when finished, it will need no further pressing. Short sample pieces can be smoothed out flat with the palms of the hand on a flat surface so that the edges are parallel and the picks lie at right angles to the warp ends. Turn them from time to time and let them dry gradually. If you pin out these small pieces be careful not to disturb the warp and weft from their positions at right angles to one another.

Fig. 25.4   Improvized drying roller

USING A DRYING ROLLER
Rolling the cloth round a slatted roller is the best way to treat longer lengths. As they are hollow they allow good circulation of air and standing them on end as the cloth slowly dries puts no pressure on any part of the cloth. The starting edge of the damp cloth is placed parallel to a slat and secured to the roller by an extra slat tied over it. While winding on the cloth, smooth it in both directions keeping the selvages level and the warp and weft at right angles to each other. Finish by tying on another stick over the end of the cloth. A roller can be improvized from a broom handle or a piece of stout plastic tubing (Fig. 25.4). This will be solid so the cloth will need reversing so that the part which was wound on first is now more open to the air. An extra long or heavy piece of cloth may need reversing even with a hollow roller. The whole process cannot be hurried and must be allowed to happen gradually.

Woollens which do not contain oil, and worsteds, do not need washing and milling. They should be damp pressed without the iron resting on or pushing across the cloth as this would disturb the ends and picks. The iron should be held just on the fabric so that the steam from the damp cloths above and below the fabric does its work.

26
Tie-and-dye, printing and painting

Dye can be applied to the warp, weft or both warp and weft, this being the most difficult. The characteristics of a tied-and-dyed design are muted colour caused by the warp and weft interlacing, rather indefinite pattern and large simple shapes. The technique does not lend itself well to designs where sharp edges and linear detail are wanted. A warp faced cloth will show up a patterned warp best (Fig. 26.1) while a weft faced cloth will do the same for a weft dyed design. Where both warp and weft are treated the areas of dyed yarns in both parts of the design must be made to interlace at the correct point.

WARP DYEING
The design must be worked out on paper first. Each unit of the design is considered and where ends can be grouped together for dyeing they can be enclosed in marking ties as the warp is made. If sections of the warp are to remain untreated, perhaps in colours which will enhance the dyed parts, these parts of the warp can be made separately so that only the band where the design is planned is on the board at one time.

A very simple way to start experimenting with tie-and-dye is to divide the warp into even sections of say 20 to 30 threads, depending on the thickness of warp yarn, and bind them individually in these groups but level with one another across the warp. Those areas of the warp which are to remain undyed must be wrapped round with strips of plastic or bound with strong fine twine to make them dye resistant.

After tying is completed the warp is washed, unless the yarn was washed before the warp was made. This is particularly necessary with woollens where there is oil in the fibre. Wash in soapy water and rinse thoroughly.

DYEING
Follow the instructions given for the dye chosen. Household dyes, which are easily obtained, are very simple to use, requiring only the addition of salt to the dye bath. For the best results use the hot water variety. Dyes can be obtained from natural sources and, used on woven textiles, make the most subtle use of the technique. Some, however, are fugitive and will fade with time. Procion dyes need no heat. Apart from a little warm water in which to dissolve the salt and soda which is added to the dye bath, the entire process is a cold water technique. There are specialist books on dyeing available. After it is tied-and-dyed this very simple arrangement can be made more complicated by pulling sections of the bound areas towards the back when tying the warp to the back beam before it is raddled. This will move the blocks back to form a checkerboard pattern. The sections of warp moved backwards are cut and tied on to the back beam and allowance must be made for this in warp length. Pulling a few threads at a time in a diagonal will make a feathered pattern when woven. Sections of untreated warps of different colours in between the tied-and-dyed blocks reduces the amount of work involved and can be used to pick up the resist colour (Fig. 26.2).

A warp faced cloth in which the warp dent is at least double the normal will show up a dyed pattern best. Woven with a thick weft the colour of the dyed areas will not be weakened by the normal interlacing of the weft, which lies between the warps.

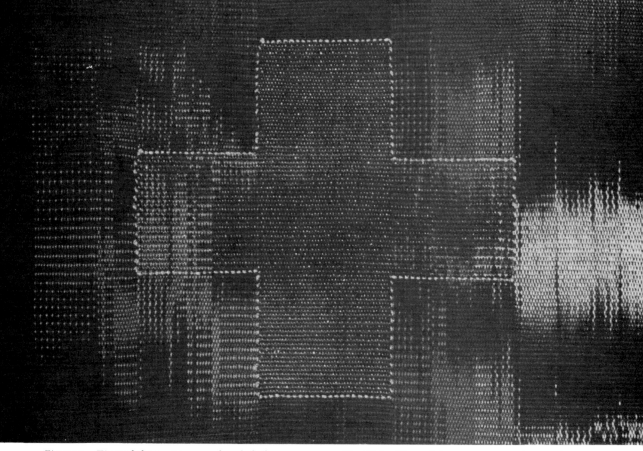

Fig. 26.1   *Tie-and-dye warp, warp faced cloth*   Fig. 26.2   *Tie-and-dye warp, warp dense set*

Fig. 26.3   Printing a warp. The loom is at the right, the warp is attached to both front and back sticks. The front stick has been detached from the loom and the warp stretched out on the table for printing, the heddle has been threaded. It can be seen on the left.

WARP PAINTING AND PRINTING

Concentrated dye can be painted directly on to the warp, sprayed on using a stencil mask, applied with a stencil brush or printed on using a screen. Small children can print with a potato. The design is either applied on to the warp before it is threaded on the loom or it can be threaded and then stretched out on a table in front of the loom, attached to the loom at one end and to the front stick at the other. Either method requires the warp to be stretched taut and taped down at intervals to cause the minimum of disturbance to the design. Profilm or paper stencils are used for the screen design (Fig. 26.3). Another way is to print a small piece of the design at a time after the warp has been threaded, printing that section of warp which is exposed between the shafts and the front beam. The batten can be removed and the reed taped to the shafts to make more space. Although this is a method which has to be done in stages, it means no design slip at all.

Tie-and-dye applied to the weft requires the use of a sample to determine the amount of take-up in one weft thread. Then the pattern is planned and the weft threads must be stretched on a board, tied in the design and dyed. After dyeing, they must be replaced in their correct order and used in that sequence.

Start with the simpler tied-and-dyed warp and consult specialist books on the more difficult techniques (Fig. 26.4).

Fig. 26.4   Painted warp, soumak

27
Appendix

TABLE LINEN

Using the frame or the simplest loom, a cross check is one interesting way of working. In the three ideas that follow, the warp order of colour is followed as a weft plan. The yarn used is a thick mercerized cotton, 2/4s or 2/6s dented singly in each hole and space in the heddle.

1. Even stripes of related colour and a neutral to produce a cross check, e.g. flame, orange, golden yellow, pale yellow, white or beige.

2. One bright or dark colour broken at intervals by a thin line of a contrasting yarn, e.g. scarlet or navy with two ends of white.

3. One colour for the warp with small sections of the ground colour and a strongly contrasting colour used end and end, e.g. royal blue, one end blue, one end white.

FOUR-SHAFT LOOM

1. Warp: 2/12s or 3/18s.

Dent: 28, two in each dent (14 dent reed), 4,3, alternating (8 dent reed).

Colour plan: Even stripes of progressive tonal difference, e.g. black, brown, dark rose, medium rose. The width of the stripe must fit the number of threads in a pattern, one, two, three or four repeats.

Pattern draft: rosepath, monk's belt, goose eye or reversed twill.

Weft: ground fabric in plain weave in one of the middle tones.

Pattern: one complete pattern in natural or white repeated to form a stripe at intervals, the yarn used double on the shuttle.

2. Warp: 2/12s or 3/18s cotton.

Dent: 28 with six empty spaces left in the reed at intervals.

Colour plan: all one colour or each section a contrast, bright or dark colour will weave equally well.

Pattern draft: twill.

Weft: one pick flat cane, one pick fine cream gimp.

Table mats and napkins are an ideal item to weave. They can be the same or form a set using slight variations of colour or pattern. Use a copper-coloured warp and alternate the weft pattern of diamonds and chevrons in black and white at the edge and in the body of the cloth (draft: reversed twill). Small pieces of cloth can be joined together with a suitable embroidery stitch.

N.B. Using a finer yarn for warp and weft makes a smoother, close fabric. 16/2s: dent 30,24/2s: dent 56,30/2s: dent 60.

Table linen can be made extra strong by using a double cloth construction. A striking set of mats could be made using the names of the members of the family in a pick-up design.

CURTAINS

1. Warp: 3/18s or 2/12s, cotton.

Dent: 14 (14 dent reed) or 16 (eight dent reed) for loose sett. For stripes of dense sett, dent double the normal number for fine cotton, 56 e.p.i. (14 dent reed is more suitable for this than an eight dent, set the warp four in each dent of the reed.)

Warp plan: narrow stripes of close denting on wider sections of the loose sett.

Colour: one colour throughout or slightly deeper tone of same colour for the dense stripe. The edge of the cloth should be dense.

Pattern draft: twill.

N.B. If the fabric is to be joined together allowance must be made for the seam on the edge stripe.

2. Warp ends can be crammed in one dent of the reed at intervals to form cords on the cloth surface. The warp plan is followed as a weft plan. Beating must be regulated to match the density of the warp denting.

3. The semi-transparent cloth can be decorated

with inlay motifs of geometric, straight-edged figures.

Warp: 2/12s or 3/18s cotton.

Dent: 14 or 16, with a 28 dent edge.

Warp plan: one natural coloured yarn.

Weft plan: the whole design motif must be worked out on squared paper and a sketch plan made of how the motifs are to repeat. The cloth is made wrong side up, the inlay placed in the same picks as the plain weave ground in the warp yarn. The inlay yarns can be a mixture of very fine yarns in wool, linen and cottons. The ground fabric makes an interesting foil for the surface texture of the inlay.

4. A totally different heavy curtaining can be made on an eight-shaft loom using a double weave block pattern or on four shafts with a summer and winter weave.

CUSHION COVERS

Like the table mats these are ideal for hand weaving. All the decorative weaves, Cleveland web, butternut and honeysuckle make interesting cushions.

Dividing a warp into three sections and using a twill running 4,3,2,1 on the right section, the middle with the twill reversed, a point twill, and the left edge, twill 1,2,3,4 makes a suitable square unit of pattern.

Any of the inlay or soumak techniques are useful for cushions.

BLANKETS

Tartans, dog tooth checks and summer and winter weave make excellent cot blankets in wool or synthetics.

1. Warp: nylon double knitting yarn.

Dent: 14.

Pattern draft: waffle.

Warp plan: white on shafts 4 and 3, pink on 1 and 2.

Weft plan: as warp, to outline the square formed in the weave. Weave 3 and 4 in the same colour as warp on shaft 3 and 4.

2. Using a double cloth with every other warp end white and different tones of soft pinks or blues paired with the white, a checked coverlet of white and pastel colour could be made (see p. 126, double cloth using a pick-up design). Tubes made in double cloth could be stuffed for extra warmth.

3. Use a lace pattern, Swedish lace, or a finger manipulated gauze weave.

DRESS FABRICS

So much depends on the fashion. Small areas of richly decorated hand weaving could be used on a bought dress length of similar weight and yarn type. Use as fine a yarn as you can if the garment has a good deal of tailoring in it. Small patterns such as twill reversed or Swedish lace can be used as cloth for dresses.

Colour is important in dress fabrics and some experiment with the basic pointed twill shape will yield exciting results. Tweeds can be made in traditional cross checks or herringbones and tartans are a good choice too. Sett 11 cut, 14–21, 16 cut, 16–22, 18 cut, 18–24. Set two threads less per 1 in (2.5 cm) where plain weave is to be used. A simple loom and coarse yarn can be used to make simple over tunics and jackets. The amount of material needed can be worked out from the paper pattern. Pin the pattern on the fabric and work a zigzag stitch on the outline before cutting. Cut up to the stitch. This is a help with a coarse cloth to prevent any unravelling of the edge, but fine cloth will not need this. Remember to make an allowance for finishing when using woollens. Washing and finishing should be done before the cloth is made up.

Bibliography

BAGS

Tapestry weave makes good heavy duty bags as does bound weave with rosepath draft (Fig. 18.2). Line the bags with a firm lining as the tapestry construction allows ends of tail combs and the like to protrude through the side of the bag. Handles can be made on tablets, or plaited and re-inforced with a strip of firm webbing or leather. A more formal bag could be made using fine cotton and a small pattern such as rosepath or goose eye. The flap of the bag could be in the pattern and the rest in plain weave. Make beach bags in double cloth with a strong pick-up design or with fringes as a decorative feature (see fig. 22.2, p. 121).

Printed or tied-and-dyed warps can be effective used with a warp-faced design. Line the beach bags with plastic.

GARDEN CHAIRS

1. Warp: 2/6s or 2/4s cotton.
Dent: 14 (14 dent reed) or 16 (8 dent reed).
Warp plan: all one colour.
Pattern draft: rosepath or herringbone.
Weft yarn: same as warp in plain weave with stripes in pattern woven in plastic raffia or thick contrasting yarn.
2. Warp: 2/6s or 2/4s cotton tied-and-dyed, sections of the warp pulled to make chevron pattern.
Dent: closer than normal to allow the design of tie-and-dye to show, 28 dent.
Weft plan: weave the back section in plain weave, the seat to be woven in a knotted cut pile.

ALBERS, A., *On Weaving*, Wesleyan University Press.

BEUTLICH, T., *The Technique of Woven Tapestry*, Batsford.

BLACK, M., *New Key to Weaving*, Bruce Publishing, Wisconsin, USA.

BOUDY, E., *The Book of Looms*, Studio Vista.

GALE, E., *From Fibres to Fabrics*, Allman.

HALSEY, M., and YOUNGMARK, L., *Foundations of Weaving*, David and Charles.

HELD, S., *Weaving*, Holt, Rinehart and Winston.

HOOPER, L., *Handloom Weaving*, Pitmans.

JOBE, J., *The Art of Tapestry*, Thames and Hudson.

KIRBY, M., *Designing on the Loom*, Studio Vista.

MURRAY, R., *Practical Modern Weaving*, Van Nostrand Reinhold.

QUARTERLY JOURNAL OF THE GUILD OF SPINNERS, WEAVERS AND DYERS.

REGENSTEINER, E., *The Art of Weaving*, Studio Vista.

SIMPSON AND WEIR, *The Weaver's Craft*, Dryad.

STEWART, E. C., *Setts of Scottish Tartans*, Oliver and Boyd.

STRAUB, M., *Hand Weaving and Cloth Design*, Pelham.

TOVEY, J., *The Technique of Weaving*, Batsford.
Weaves and Pattern Drafting, Batsford.

WIEGLE, P., *Double Weaves*, Pitmans.

Glossary

Apron: strong material attached to the back and front of the loom to which the warp is tied.

Apron sticks: warp sticks in the seam of the apron.

Batten: the pivotted frame which carries the reed.

Beam (cloth): the front roller on which the cloth is wound as it is woven.

Beam (warp): the back roller on which the warp is wound.

Beaming: winding or rolling the warp on to the cloth beam.

Binder: plain weave used between each pattern pick in overshot drafts.

Block: a unit of design using so many threads in a draft.

Bobbin: a small spool or quill used in a roller shuttle.

Bobbin winder: a turning spindle used in filling a bobbin for a roller shuttle.

Chain: the warp removed from the board and twisted in a crochet chain to shorten it for storage.

Cheese: a package of yarn.

Choke ties: lengths of yarn tied round the warp to secure its order.

Cone: a conical shaped package of yarn, free standing.

Cop: cylindrical package of yarn supported on a rod (the yarn unwinds from the top in cones and cops).

Countershed: the second shed formed.

Cramming: increasing the normal density of warp or weft threads in a weave.

Cross: the crossing of warp threads which can be single or in groups; it maintains the order of the warp.

Cross sticks: sticks placed in the warp to keep the cross in its correct order. The sticks are tied together through the holes in each end.

Cut: 300 yards in Galashiels count.

Dent: one space between the teeth of a reed.

Denting: the density of the warp ends in the reed, the number of spaces to a given measure in the reed.

Double weave: a weave which makes two layers of cloth at the same time.

Draft: a diagrammatic plan of the threading order and the sequence of shedding.

Draw down: a representation on squared paper of the way in which the warp and weft intersect to make the cloth.

Dressing the loom: all preparatory stages in loom preparation prior to weaving.

Drying roller: a slatted roller on which washed cloth is rolled to dry.

Dukagång: a Scandinavian weave in which a decorative yarn floats over three warp ends and is tied down by the fourth.

End: one warp thread.

Entering: threading the heddles.

Eye: the wire loop through which the warp is put in a heddle.

Fell: the edge of the cloth formed by the last pick woven.

Felting: matting together of woollen fibres caused by milling.

Fibre: a material which can be spun into a yarn.

Filament: a continuous yarn as that produced by a silk worm.

Finishing: a process such as washing, milling, crabbing through which cloth goes after removal from the loom.

Float: a thread passing over two or more threads of the opposite threads.

Harness: see shaft.

Heading: the small piece of weaving done at the start of work on a loom.

Heddle: a wire or string loop with a small eye in

the middle, which holds a warp end, so that when the shaft is raised, the heddle raises the warp end also.

Lease: another name for the cross in a warp.

Leash: a loop of string used to make the countershed when using a shed stick to make the first shed, often used with a leash rod.

Milling: the process of expanding and matting the fibres in woollen cloth by working the cloth in hot soapy water.

Mounting: the complete mechanism of a loom.

Pawl: the movable metal tongue which falls into the rachet wheel to stop the beam on the loom from turning.

Pick: one row of weaving, coming from the idea that the warps are picked up when woven.

Pile: loops or cut threads at right angles to the cloth surface.

Pirn: yarn package with the yarn unwinding from one end.

Ply: two or more threads of yarn twisted together.

Porrey cross: the singles cross on a warp used for entering the warp through the heddles.

Portee cross: the coarse cross on a warp used for raddling the warp.

Quill: a small core of a bobbin originally made from a reed or a feather.

Race: the ledge on a beater on which the shuttle runs when using a roller shuttle.

Rachet wheel: a toothed wheel used with a pawl to control the tension on a loom.

Raddle: a wooden comb with a removable top and pegs placed at even intervals. It is used to space the warp to its correct width for rolling on to the loom.

Reed: a metal frame with evenly spaced teeth, known as dents, used for spacing the warp, and, in conjunction with the beater, used to beat in the weft.

Reed hook: a flat fish-shaped metal hook used for threading the reed.

Rigid heddle: a frame, with alternating holes and spaces, used to divide the warp into the sheds and to beat in the weft on a simple loom.

Roller: see beam.

Scouring: removing the oil from woollen cloth by washing in hot soapy water.

Selvage: the self-edge of the cloth formed by the weft returning round the warp ends.

Sett: the density of warp and weft threads in a given measurement of cloth. To set is the verb.

Setting up: the complete process of threading, sleying the reed and tying up ready to weave on a loom.

Shaft: a frame made of metal or wood on which the heddles are suspended.

Shed: the triangular space made when the two layers of the warp divide through which the shuttle carrying the weft thread is passed.

Shed stick: a wide stick inserted under every other warp on a frame loom which, when turned on its edge will create a wide enough space to pass the weft thread.

Shot: one pick of weft, one passage of the shuttle.

Shuttle: the implement used to carry the weft yarn through the shed and weave.

Singles: one unplied yarn.

Sley: entering the warps through the reed.

Spool: a cylindrical package of yarn.

Spool rack: a wooden frame with removable steel rods used to support spools of yarn which unwind by revolving.

Sticks, cross: used to secure the cross, these are wider than the warp sticks and have holes in their ends through which they can be tied together.

Sticks, warp: narrow sticks used to interleave the layers of warp on the back roller and to tie the

Suppliers

warp to the apron at the back and front of the loom.

Sword: a stick used to beat the weft in.

Tabby: plain weave.

Take-up: the amount a warp and weft contract by the action of the opposite threads bending over each other in the weave.

Threading: putting the warp through the heddles using a threading hook.

Twist: the yarn spin, the direction of the fibres in the spin resemble the centre of a letter S or Z.

Warp: the threads in cloth which are stretched lengthwise on a frame or loom, so that the weft can be interlaced with them to make a fabric.

Warp faced: a cloth in which the warp predominates on the top surface of the cloth.

Warping: making a continuous loop of yarn of a certain length and containing the required number of ends.

Warping board, pegs, mill: see section on warping in text.

Weave: the order of interlacing warp and weft yarns to make a cloth.

Weft: the yarns which interlace across the warp to form cloth.

Weft faced: a cloth in which the weft predominates in the top surface.

Winding on: see beaming.

Yarn: fibres which have been spun.

Yarn count: the classification of yarns by their thickness, length and weight.

LOOMS AND ACCESSORIES

Harris Looms, Emmerich (Berlon) Ltd., Wotton Road, Ashford, Kent.

Dryad, Northgates, Leicester.

Eliza Leadbetter, Rookery Cottage, Daleford's Lane, Whitegate, near Northwich, Cheshire.

YARNS

William Hall and Co. (Monsall) Ltd., 177 Stanley Road, Cheadle Hulme, Cheadle, Cheshire.

The Handweaver's Gallery, 29 Haroldstone Road, London E17.

Yarns, 17a Hastings Road, Bexhill-on-Sea, East Sussex TN40 2BC.

Texere Yarns, College Mill, Barkerend Road, Bradford, West Yorkshire BD3 9AQ.

Craftsman's Mark Ltd., Trefnant, Denbign, North Wales LL16 5UD.

Jackson's Rug Centre, Croft Mill, Hebden Bridge, Yorkshire.

T. M. Hunter Ltd., Sutherland Wool Mills, Brora, Scotland.

J. Hyslop Bathgate and Co., Island Street, Galashiels, Scotland.

J. McAndrew and Son Ltd., Battinson Road Mills, Queen's Road, Halifax.

Dryad, Northgates, Leicester.

Index